ATHEISM
IN THE ENGLISH RENAISSANCE

ATHEISM
IN THE
ENGLISH
RENAISSANCE

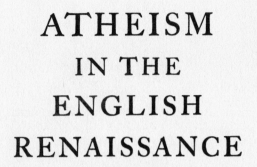

GEORGE T. BUCKLEY

New York
RUSSELL & RUSSELL
1965

To

CHARLES READ BASKERVILL

INTRODUCTION

THOMAS NASHE would have no champion against atheism unless he had first run over infinite labyrinths of books and become familiar with the confessions of all philosophers. Now it is not my purpose to combat atheists but to write a history of their devious devices as they were related by Renaissance clerics and moralists; yet I cannot but be conscious of the fact that I have not altogether met Nashe's high requirements. If as a result of this my study falls short of what the critical reader could desire, I can at least plead a few extenuating circumstances. In the first place, I have been engaged in a field usually regarded as almost barren of philosophical thought. Scholasticism had broken down and the new philosophy was not to begin until the time of Bacon and Descartes. Lying between these events the sixteenth century, preserving some fragments of the old system and disturbed by strivings toward the new, torn by religious struggles and filled with the multifarious activity of the Renaissance, had no unity of thought and no settled philosophical system. For the historian of religion, or politics, or literature it is a rich period, but it has been largely neglected by historians of philosophy. Consequently, with few predecessors to guide me, I have had to play the part of a pioneer, at least as far as English thought is concerned, and have not been able to go forward with the boldness and confidence of those who walk beaten paths.

Again, I have attempted to trace a movement in thought, the reaction to religious unbelief, through an entire century, to survey a whole body of literature, and naturally have not been able to treat any phase of the subject in the exhaustive manner that a more narrow method of approach would require. This being so, of course I do not regard my findings as conclusive and consider no question that I have treated as closed. I have meant to indicate general lines of inquiry, to suggest methods of approach, to give some idea of the nature and extent of the subject and the material available—in short, to map out a field which future investigators will, I trust, explore more thoroughly.

A word in regard to the general plan of my study seems necessary: The first four chapters are to be regarded as introductory. In these I attempt to fill in the background for whatever irreligious thought the age may have produced, to point to the main sources for religious unbelief. For this method I confess some indebtedness to the splendid work of Henri Busson, *Les sources et le développement du rationalisme dans la littérature française*, who has employed it so successfully in his study of rationalism in French literature during the same period. Indeed, what I have to say about classical sources and the thought of the Paduan school is little more than the treatment of English literature in the way that M. Busson had already treated French, although I have not scrupled to dissent from him when I think I find him in error. I ought in fairness to myself to say that his method is so obvious that I should no doubt have hit upon it for myself before pursuing my studies very far, but he at any rate deserves the credit of suggesting it to me. For the chapter on Machiavellianism I have found other works more helpful, particularly Charbonnel's *La pensée italienne au XVIᵉ siècle*, and the chapter on the religious sects is largely my own.

In these four chapters I have indicated and reviewed the main sources for religious unbelief, but of course have not meant that they were the only ones. An atheist can find atheism anywhere. There were other sources, such as the rise of the new science, Pyrrhonism, and perhaps the book *De tribus impostoribus*, but these I regard as of minor importance and have reserved them for consideration until it was necessary to call attention to them in connection with the reaction.

For the study of the reaction itself, which forms the main body of my work, I have found Friedrich Brie's article, "Deismus und Atheismus in der englischen Renaissance,"[1] very help-

[1] *Anglia*, XLVIII (1928), 54–98, 105–68.

ful, especially for bibliography. Herr Brie's study is an important one, and no student of free thought in this or any later period ought to be ignorant of it. Yet it is not without its defects. In attempting to handle a subject of such scope in the compass of a single article, Brie has been able to write only what may be described as a series of disconnected notes rather than a well-rounded and integrated study. The background of English unbelief, the possible sources, the relation to the thought of France—these and other topics essential to an understanding of the subject he has of necessity had to omit. Moreover, Brie's main interest is in the eighteenth century, and he has been more concerned to discover the origins of deism and other phases of eighteenth-century thought than he has to study the thought of the Renaissance for its own sake. I have tried to improve upon this method and in addition have brought to bear on the subject a number of important works which Brie did not consider.

Finally, I have thought it fitting after so extended a study of religious unbelief to consider somewhat in detail the two cases of atheism most often brought to our attention, those of Christopher Marlowe and Sir Walter Raleigh. There is no lack of studies on the atheism of these two men, and especially on that of Marlowe, as a glance at my footnotes will show, but I have not hesitated to go over some fairly well-known material in order to round out my own study. Any contribution I have made to this part of the subject has been the result of my unwillingness to consider the atheism of Marlowe and Raleigh as an isolated phenomenon; hence I have tried to analyze their unbelief and to discover from whence they had drawn it. With Marlowe I fear that my success will be regarded as dubious, but with Raleigh I think that I can modestly claim to have added some new material and to have illuminated some aspects of the matter that have hitherto escaped attention.

TABLE OF CONTENTS

I

Classical Sources

THE conflict between pagan culture and Christianity did not begin with the Renaissance. It began with the first meeting of the two, when the Christian missionaries broadened their activities to include the gentile world. The conflict was inherent in the nature of the two systems, it was fully expected, and it was already under way when the apostle Paul said, "We preach Christ crucified, unto the Jews a stumbling-block, and unto the Greeks foolishness." In the bitter and internecine struggle that developed the Christians finally triumphed, but the *Götterdämmerung* brought no cessation of hostilities. Among the early Fathers, Cyril, Origin, Lactantius, and Augustine laid on with a will. Nothing would satisfy them, it seemed, except the extirpation of the last vestiges of classical culture, and this they were not quite able to accomplish, although the Dark Ages that immediately ensued may testify in some part how nearly they came to their goal.

During the Middle Ages, of course, the attitude of the church to pagan literature superficially appeared to change somewhat, but essentially it was about the same. A number of writers whose works had not been lost or forgotten, notably Ovid and Terence, remained on the prohibited list, and when his works began to be rediscovered to Western Europe around 1200, even Aristotle found himself so ranged. But not for long. Alexander of Hales, Albertus Magnus, and other doctors set themselves the difficult task of harmonizing Aristotle with Christian dogma, and with the great work of Thomas Aquinas the task was regarded as practically complete. Plato, Seneca (with the exception of the dramas), and Cicero (with the exception of *De natura deorum* and *De divinatione*) were easier to adjust to the Christian system. Thus the matter stood at the end of the Middle Ages. The pagan writers who could not be reconciled to Christian thought were, as minions of Satan, to be accursed and damned and if possible run to earth and slain. Those who could be reconciled were to be regarded, in spite of some trifling and easily pardonable divergencies of thought, not as pagans at all, but as forerunners of Christianity and almost the equals of the early Church Fathers.

The Renaissance, it has often been insisted, was no sudden and complete breaking with the past. Nevertheless I suppose no one will deny that a change of some kind, no matter how slow and gradual, took place in England say between the years 1400 and 1600. This change that we call the Renaissance is difficult to define, its cause is difficult to discover,[1] and no small part of the difficulty lies in the fact that it dealt not with things, not with men or nations, but with ideas, that it was a readjustment of values, a new way of looking at things, rather than any change in the things themselves. It began to be borne in upon the minds of men, so long darkened, that this world itself and its affairs are worthy of the attention of the best men and that man himself is not unworthy of study. Thus there gradually came to be a shift of interest to this world as opposed to the hereafter and to the individual as opposed to the church or state. In its larger aspects the Renaissance then may be regarded as the secularization of men's minds. Specifically in regard to the classics men began to be aware that Plato and Aristotle were not forerunners of Christ, but representatives of a religion and culture in which Christ and his church had no part. This was the secularization of the classics. They now came to be read for themselves and as literature, and when so read the classical revival had begun.

Since the entire Renaissance tended toward secularization, and since the classics began to be understood as the thought of

[1] Witness the popular error that it was caused by the fall of Constantinople in 1453.

an alien religion, it is apparent that a man in sympathy with these movements would find the reading of almost any piece of Greek or Latin literature an experience not likely to make him a sounder Christian. The classics might make him a better moralist or a keener philosopher, and some of them might seem superficially to be bolstering up his Christianity, but the event was to show that good moralists and keen philosophers were not always good Christians, and that Christianity supported by pagan thought developed a disconcerting tendency to be neither paganism nor Christianity, but a new thing that was known in the course of time as natural religion or "deism."[2] Aside from the moral works of antiquity, however, and aside from the great body of pure literature, most of which had little religious significance, there was in addition a considerable body of works of a skeptical, inquiring nature—works which clearly had an agnostic if not an atheistical import and which could not be reconciled to the tenets of Christianity.

A line cannot of course be drawn definitely around this group, for the works of some writers fall partly on one side and partly on the other. Cicero, for example, was universally praised for his *De amicitia* and *De senectute*, but he had also written *De natura deorum* and *De divinatione*. Plutarch had written his *Morals* and his *Lives*, but he had much to be pardoned for in his *Cessation of the Oracles* and *Isis and Osiris*. And even Aristotle's *De anima* continued by some to be regarded with suspicion. But there were nevertheless a few who were unequivocally skeptical in the main body of their works and whose skepticism was not relieved by other works more pleasing to Christian ears. Chief among these were Pliny, Lucian, and Lucretius, and these we shall first consider.

It should perhaps first be said to avoid misunderstanding

[2] A movement already under way in France by 1560. See the Preface to Pierre Viret's *Exposition de la doctrine de la foy Chrestienne* (Geneva, 1564). It was given fairly clear expression by Jean Bodin in his *Colloquium Heptaplomeres* (1588; ed. Roger Chauvire, Paris, 1914), and in England by Lord Herbert of Cherbury in his *De veritate* (written *ca.* 1619 but first printed at Paris in 1624; London, 1645), but of course it did not reach its full development until the first half of the eighteenth century.

that the purpose here is only to show *possible* sources for religious unbelief in the Renaissance. It cannot definitely be stated that this or that person became an unbeliever from reading
Lucian's dialogues or Cicero's *Nature of the Gods*, but it can be
said with confidence that the skeptics of classical antiquity were
one of the major sources for religious doubt in sixteenth-century
England. The purpose here, then, is to show what writers were
most likely to cause that doubt, to review their teachings briefly, and to cite from their works the most important passages in
point.

One of the favorite books of the Renaissance was the *Natural
History* of Caius Plinius Secundus, a work that went through
thirty-eight editions on the Continent between 1469 and 1532.
Even in England it enjoyed better fortune than the works of
any other skeptic, being three times reprinted before 1600. This
popularity no doubt was largely caused by the fascination
Pliny's monsters, rare herbs, marvelous plants, and other wonders had for the Renaissance mind, for with allusions to these
the literature of the period is full. Of this pseudo-natural history Pliny's agnosticism, to be sure, forms only a small part, being confined to two chapters, one in Book II and the other in
Book VII, but it is both intense and pessimistic. There is no
God, says Pliny, unless it is the world itself, and if there is one
his powers are limited, he has no providence over the lives of
men, being employed on weighty business of his own, and he has
no concern with our trivial affairs. The soul is not immortal and
man will be after his death just as he was before his birth. And
in a famous passage Pliny declares that the state of man is be-
low that of beasts, as he, unlike them, is born helpless, under-
goes a long period of infancy, never attains much bodily vigor,
and is without the natural means of defense with which all
animals are provided. Surely the world is our cruel stepmother
and there can be no beneficent, all-powerful God watching over
us.

Like Aristotle, Pliny declared the world to be immortal or
eternal, thereby offending the Christians, who looked backward

to the creation and forward to the last judgment. Like many another skeptic, he judged the idea of providence to be a delusion, and like free spirits of all ages, he asserted the expediency of religious belief in a state for purely political reasons:

Howbeit, the beleefe in these matters that the gods haue care of mens estate, is good, expedient, and profitable in the course of this life: as also that the vengeance and punishment of malefactors may well come late (whiles God is busily occupied otherwise in so huge a frame of the world) but neuer misseth in the end.[3]

Nothing could be more nauseous to devout Christians than such a compromise with Satan, as can be seen in the storm of protest that greeted Machiavelli's similar proposal.

Much better known in the Renaissance for his attitude toward religion and superstition was the Greek satirist Lucian, the bold, cynical thinker who undertook to laugh men out of their folly and from whose ridicule even the gods of Olympus were not safe. Among the Humanists he had enjoyed a considerable vogue, for they like Lucian were beset on all sides with ignorance, superstition, and blind credulity, which they dared not attack directly, but against which they hoped to prevail by means of satire and ridicule. Erasmus had helped to popularize him by including a number of his thoughts in *Adagia* (1501), and his influence is easily noted in the *Colloquies* and *Praise of Folly* and in France in the works of Rabelais, Des Periers, and Tahureau. Already Lucian's *Dialogues* had been translated into Latin by Erasmus and More in 1506, and were several times printed in England, once by Wynkyn de Worde in 1528 and once by Siberch at Cambridge in 1521 during the short time the printing press was in operation there. But after 1530, whether because of the settling-down of the Reformation, or because from about that time on the classics began to be read for content as much as for models of style and more attention was thus paid to his attitude toward religion, Lucian came into great disfavor, and his works were not printed again in England until

[3] I have used the second (1635) edition of Philemon Holland's translation of 1601, p. 5.

1634. Nevertheless with the impetus given his works by Erasmus and with the numerous editions on the Continent, there is no doubt that Lucian's writings were easily available to anyone who wished to read them.

In philosophy Lucian seems to have been an Epicurean. As might be expected from this, he had no belief in the supernatural, but his main characteristic was a hatred of sham, hypocrisy, and miracle-working, a hatred so great that it colored practically everything he wrote. These two things, his contempt for miracle-workers and his love for Epicurus, whom in one place he declared to be "the thinker who grasped the nature of things and was in solitary possession of the truth,"[4] would alone of course have rendered Lucian anathema to all good Christians.

Lucian is perhaps at his best, however, in the *Dialogues of the Gods*, a series of rapier-like attacks on the Olympians for their human passions, amours, inconsistencies, and anthropomorphic natures in general. The legends are told in straightforward prose, with the poetic glamour and reverence stripped off; the gods are spoken of as human beings and consequently become ridiculous. Now the scoffing tone adopted by Lucian in speaking of the gods may perhaps in his own day have served to turn people from paganism to Christianity, as the Messrs. Fowler opine,[5] but in the Renaissance, when Christianity was no longer as pure as it had once been, and when it found itself under a searching scrutiny not from pagans but from its own members, there was more likelihood that the thought would occur to the keener wits of the time that Lucian's remarks could be applied without much change to the Christian deity himself. For instance, there is a passage in *Timon the Misanthrope*, in which Zeus is mocked for his senility and lack of former vigor, that because of its reference to the flood could hardly escape this application:

Why, in Deucalion's time, hey presto, everything was swamped, mankind went under, and just one little ark was saved, standing on the top of Lycoreus

4 *The Works of Lucian*, trans. H. W. and F. G. Fowler (Clarendon Press, 1905), II, 224.

5 *Ibid.*, Introd., p. xxvi.

and preserving a remnant of human seed for the generation of greater wickedness. . . . . If anyone offers you a victim or a garland nowadays . . . . he does it not because he thinks it is any good, but because he may as well keep up an old custom. It will not be long, most glorious of deities, before they serve you as you served Cronus, and depose you.[6]

If anyone were so obtuse as not to make the application here, Lucian in other places left him no alternative, for Christianity itself, then just beginning to take root in the Empire, did not escape his darts. In *The Liar*, written against all who believe in miracles, apparitions, and the supernatural, he mentions a number of impostors, among them a "Syrian adept from Palestine," by whom he almost certainly means Christ:

I need not enlarge on the subject: just look at that Syrian adept from Palestine: every one knows how time after time he has found a man thrown down on the ground in a lunatic fit, foaming at the mouth and rolling his eyes: and how he got him on his feet again and sent him away in his right mind; and a handsome fee he takes for freeing men from such horrors.[7]

In *The Death of Peregrine* we are told how the magician Protus once associated himself with the Christians:

It was now that he came across the priests and scribes of the Christians, in Palestine, and picked up their queer creed. I can tell you, he pretty soon convinced them of his superiority; prophet, elder, ruler of the synagogue—he was everything at once. . . . . They took him for a God, accepted his laws, and declared him their president. The Christians, you know, worship a *man* to this day,—the distinguished personage who introduced their novel rites, and was crucified on that account.[8]

Lucian was more than a mere model of style for the Humanists, the suggester of a certain tone they should take toward stupidity and folly. He was pregnant with possibilities for an active rationalism, and the fact was well recognized by the moralists, who coined the term Lucianist to fit the scoffing, blasphemous type of atheist so often mentioned in the late sixteenth century. But one feels that even this feature of Lucian's work, dominant though it was, was a little too much emphasized. For, in spite of his mocking tone, his works were marked by a clarity of thought, sanity, and common sense that could not fail to

[6] *Op. cit.*, I, 32.

[7] *Op. cit.*, III, 239.   [8] *Op. cit.*, IV, 82.

recommend him to all rational minds. "Truth and good sense," says Lucian: "these are the drugs of our ailments; let us employ them, and that empty thing, a lie, need have no terror for us."

More aggressive in tone and more thoroughgoing in his religious unbelief than even Lucian was the Latin poet Lucretius, the disciple of Epicurus and the author of the brilliant poem *De rerum natura*. Mr. Preserved Smith says wittily:

Philosophy is like a climber on the Mer de Glace, tied in the middle of a rope at either end of which is a guide. One of these guides is the scientist, a daring and active man ever pressing forward vigorously to new and untried ground; the other is Mrs. Grundy, a staid and cautious individual, heavily ballasted with the *mores* and traditions of the group, and extremely slow in her movements. For this reason the trail of philosophy is always parallel to that of science; the same ground is covered, only more slowly, and more reluctantly.[9]

Lucretius cut the rope between him and Mrs. Grundy and pressed forward closely on the heels of his foremost guide. For with meager scientific information, and most of that incorrect, he nevertheless reached at many points practically the same conclusions as modern philosophy, that is to say, a scientific, materialistic conception of the universe and agnosticism.

At the base of the philosophy of Lucretius was the atom, an infinitely small body or seed (*semina*) of which all matter was composed. The universe was created by a fortuitous falling together of these atoms, the heavy ones sinking to the bottom and making the earth, the light ones remaining above and forming the air and the heavens. The universe thus accidentally created was ruled only by natural law. It was a kind of machine, not unlike that of Descartes if the mathematics were left out, and everything in it, including man himself, was the result of the operation of these natural laws, for on it the supernatural had never impinged.

In spite of this, however, Lucretius did believe in the existence of the gods, but he would remove them to some place infinitely remote where they were in perfect ease and tranquillity and intent only on their own happiness. To him the idea that these gods, supremely content as they were, created the world for man, and that they had any concern in his welfare, was outside the bounds of all credulity. He says:

> But now to say this spacious World began
> By bounteous Heaven, contriv'd to pleasure Man;
> And therefore this vast Frame they toil'd to raise,
> And fit for Us, should meet with equal praise. . . . .
> 'Tis fond. For what could Man return again?
> What profit to the Gods for all their pain,
> That they should work for him? Why break their rest,
> In which they liv'd before secure and blest?[10]

Like Pliny, Lucretius took an extremely pessimistic view of the state of man in this world. It is clear to him that the world was never designed for man at all, and to prove this he advanced the conventional arguments against the doctrine of divine Providence. Most of the world is water, great stretches of it are either too hot or too cold for man's habitation, and what is left is often broken up by mountain ranges. Even the parts which man can inhabit do not produce food for him except with the greatest reluctance, and if Nature were left to herself, her only harvests would be briars and weeds. If the world were made for man, why the droughts and storms that destroy the results of his toil? Why the savage beasts lying in wait to slay him? Why plagues and sickness in all seasons? Like Pliny he is drawn to the conclusion that the world is better adapted to beasts than to man.

As might be expected from what has already been said, Lucretius denied the immortality of the soul in emphatic terms. Following Epicurus, he taught that the soul, like all other matter, was composed of atoms, although of very small, round atoms of a much finer texture than those that made up grosser substances. But it was none the less material, and as further proofs of its mortality he points out that it grows old with the body, that it is touched by all the ills of the flesh, that it could have no existence apart from the body, since it is dependent on

---

[10] P. 144. I have used Thomas Creech's translation, *Titus Lucretius Carus: His Six Books of Epicurean Philosophy* (London, 1683), in my opinion the best verse translation ever made.

the five senses, and that the dread of death indicates that the soul itself is aware of its mortality.

More than any other rationalist of antiquity Lucretius was conscious of his position as an enemy of religion. His attack against the gods did not consist of a few almost parenthetical statements as did Pliny's, nor was it confined to a minor work or two and then stated somewhat equivocally as was Plutarch's and Cicero's. It was bold and direct and it dominated his whole work. He exulted in his freedom, and his most eloquent passages were in praise of Epicurus for delivering mankind from religious fear:

> Not the fam'd stories of the Deity,
> Not all the Thunder of the threatning Sky
> Could stop his rising Soul; thro all he past,
> The strongest bounds that powerful Nature cast:
> His vigorous and active Mind was hurl'd
> Beyond the flaming limits of this World
> Into the mighty Space, and there did see
> How things begin, what can, what cannot be;
> How all must die, all yield to fatal force,
> What steddy limits bound their natural course;
> He saw all this, and brought it back to us.
> Wherefore by his success our Right we gain,
> Religion is our Subject, and we reign.[11]

There is no doubt that thoughts such as these made a profound impression on the Renaissance mind. Lucretius was widely known and read throughout Europe during the sixteenth century, especially of course in Italy and France, but also in England. His poem appears never to have been printed in England until the translation of Thomas Creech in 1683, but as early as 1473 it had been printed by Ferandus of Brescia, and there were dozens of editions in France and Italy during the next hundred years. That Lucretianism was spreading rapidly in England as well as in France[12] is well attested by the vigorous replies to his philosophy by Sir Philip Sidney, Sir John Davies, and John

[11] *Op. cit.*, pp. 3-4.

[12] Montaigne may serve as an illustration of how far it had gone in France, for he had read Lucretius with a vengeance. I have counted 148 quotations from him in the *Essays*, many of them as much as ten or twelve lines in length.

Davies of Hereford, and by the popularity of the works of Du Bartas, Mornay, and La Primaudaye on both sides of the channel.

Marcus Tullius Cicero, the darling of the Renaissance, reached his great popularity for two main reasons. First, he was selected as a model of style. His extravagant, slightly ornate rhetoric seemed to the Humanists to rise to the greatest heights of which the Latin language was capable. Second, he was a sober, well-balanced moralist, a man who expressed eminently correct sentiments about a vast number of things. But the versatile Tully was not easy to pigeonhole. He was never a particularly deep thinker and is hardly to be ranked with the philosophers, but what he lacked in profundity he made up for in catholicity and cosmopolitanism. Like Aristotle he had an oar in all waters, and it is not surprising that he did not always confine himself to opinions that Christians could share. He did so in *De officiis* and *Paradoxa stoicorum*, and these received the unqualified approval of the Humanists, but from the beginning Christians had regarded *De natura deorum* and *De divinatione* with suspicion.

De natura deorum is a debate between three men, Velleius the Epicurean, Balbus the Stoic, and Cotta, the opponent of both, about two important points in religion, the existence and nature of the gods, and miracles. Ostensibly Cicero is merely a listener anxious to learn and taking no part in the discussion, but the reader is not likely to forget that Cicero is writing the arguments for all three and allowing the use of *reductio ad absurdum* in a strongly rationalistic way, ridiculing, in fact, the very arguments the Christians used to prove their own mysteries. Mr. A. S. Pease regards *De natura deorum* as an attempt to give in an impartial manner the beliefs of the different schools and thinks the work was meant to be a kind of religious encyclopedia.[13] It may have been so, but whatever side Cicero took or whether

[13] "The Conclusions of Cicero's *De natura deorum*," *Transactions of the American Philological Association*, XLIV (1913), 25-37.

any at all is irrelevant. The point to be emphasized is that he treated religious mysteries in a rationalistic way, just as if they were to be tested by reason and not accepted on pure faith. To be sure, he was speaking of the pagan gods, but at no time were the Christians so blind as not to recognize that an argument that can disprove the existence of one god can disprove that of another.

One passage that must have appealed with especial force to Christians of the sixteenth century after the Reformation had to do with the variety of religions. Now we know from other sources that the coming of the sects to England and the religious quarrel in general were regarded as one of the main causes of atheism there. To people whom the spectacle of numerous sects all claiming to be the sole legatees of divine truth had made skeptical, the statement of Cicero must have come as the final word of authority. He says concerning religions:

> There is no subject on which the learned, as well as the unlearned, differ so strenuously as this; and since their opinions are so various, and so repugnant one to another, it is possible that none of them may be, and absolutely impossible that more than one should be right.[14]

This, it should be added, was the opinion of Cicero himself, expressed before Velleius, Balbus, and Cotta began their discussion.

Two arguments of the Stoics for the existence of God that had been taken over by the Christians and reiterated countless times, especially during the sixteenth century, were that natural order in the universe proclaimed a divine ruler and that his existence was proved by the universal consent of mankind, savage as well as civilized. Balbus, the Stoic in *De natura deorum*, develops both of them fully. He points to the regularity of the heavenly bodies, to the return of night and day, to the recurrence of the seasons, to the presence of natural law in the world, in short to the fact that the universe is a cosmos and not chaos, and says this is clear proof of a directing power. But Cotta

---

[14] *Of the Nature of the Gods and Divinations*, ed. and trans. C. D. Younge (London, 1907), p. 3.

brushes all this aside by saying that these effects are to be explained by reason, and that those who point to them as evidence
for the existence of a deity are merely impeaching their own
ability to discover natural causes. And to the argument from
universal consent Cotta considers it sufficient to reply that "the
question is, not whether there are people who believe there are
gods, but whether there are gods or not."

Cicero had left some uncertainty as to his own views in *De
natura deorum*, as Augustine says,[15] but in *De divinatione* he announced himself boldly enough. This is an argument between
Cicero and his brother Quintus on the matter of divinations and
miracles, Quintus speaking first and endeavoring to support
their reality, and Cicero refuting him by assigning everything
to natural causes. Quintus had somewhat absurdly instanced
the fact of a mule's having given birth to a colt as a proof of
miracles. Cicero answered:

You have mentioned a wonderful story of a mule that was delivered of a
colt; a strange event, because of its extreme rarity. But . . . . whatever is
born, of whatever kind it may be, must have some cause in nature. . . . .
Investigate, if you can, the natural cause of every novel and extraordinary
circumstance: even if you cannot discover the cause, still you may feel sure
that nothing can have taken place without a cause; and, by the principles of
nature, drive away the terror which the novelty of the thing may have occasioned in you. Then neither earthquakes, nor thunderstorms, nor showers
of blood and stones, nor shooting stars, nor glancing torches will alarm you
any more.[16]

Compared to the advanced opinions of Lucretius and Pliny,
Cicero's rationalism of course was rather mild, but what there
was of it must have been well-nigh universally known, such was
the popularity of his works. The tag "as Tullie sayeth" meets
the eye on almost every page of the essays and treatises of the
period. Sir Thomas Elyot, for example, in *The Governour* gives
sixty-three separate quotations from Cicero, the most from any
author, Aristotle coming next with twenty-four, and Ascham in
Toxophilus twenty-three from Cicero, Aristotle coming next
with eighteen. These two authors, chosen at random, probably

[15] *The City of God*, V, 9.   [16] *Op. cit.*, pp. 220, 224.

represent very fairly the estimation in which Cicero was held, and thus it is evident that whatever rationalistic qualities were in his works must have received the fullest possible opportunity for development in England.

It is more than a mere conjecture, however, that Cicero's works could develop unbelief in his admirers, and as proof we may glance for a moment at the career of the French Humanist, Etienne Dolet, who perhaps better than any other man, certainly than any Englishman, shows Ciceronianism at its fullest development. He it was who replied with the greatest scurrility to Erasmus' *Ciceronianus* with his *De imitatione Ciceroniana* in 1534, and he it was of whom John Odoni said:

> At Lyons he repeated this saying to me, "Let others choose other masters, I approve only of Christ and Tully; Christ and Tully are sufficient for me." I saw nothing of Christ, however, in his hands or in his books; God knows whether he has anything in his heart.[17]

Dolet was certainly incredulous about many points of Christian dogma. In his poems he spoke doubtfully of immortality, referring to death as a quiet sleep, and in *Commentariorum linguae latinae* he even advanced the opinion that there was no immortality except glory or renown, a lasting name, such as Cicero's or Caesar's.

In 1542 he was arrested at Lyons, where he was then living, for using *Habeo fidem* instead of *Credo* in a poetical version of the creed, with omitting the words *Communionem sanctorum*, and with employing the word *Fatum* in a heathen sense. For this he was condemned to death, but was pardoned by Francis I. In 1546 he was again arrested on similar charges, particularly for translating a passage in the pseudo-Platonic piece *Axiochus* with the words "après la mort tu ne seras plus rien du tout," and this time was burned at the stake, to the applause of both Catholics and Protestants. There may of course have been some other influence at work in developing Dolet's unbelief, but if so it was not especially evident, and his state of mind and his

---

[17] Quoted by R. C. Christie in *Etienne Dolet, the Martyr of the Renaissance* (London, 1880), p. 216.

death appear to have been due almost entirely to too great an admiration for Cicero.

Dolet is cited only as an example of what Ciceronianism carried to its extreme limit would produce. The English disciples of the great orator were not disposed to go so far, but even they were not likely to have been unaware of the fact that Cicero, in addition to his moral teaching, contained many thoughts capable of developing religious unbelief in his readers.

Plutarch in a number of respects was quite similar to Cicero in regard to moral teachings and religious incredulity. His moral and practical treatises, much read among the Humanists and indeed throughout the century, together with the *Lives*, form the main body of his works, and these contained nothing at which Christians could take offense. But *The Cessation of the Oracles* and *Isis and Osiris* dealt with miracles, a point fundamental to both pagan and Christian religious systems, and toward miracles Plutarch took a strongly rationalistic attitude, explaining them entirely by natural causes. These treatises seem, however, not to have been known to any extent until Amyot's translation of the *Œuvres morales* in 1572, and by that time their ideas had already been made common by Cicero.

His work *On Superstition* merits a word or two because of the favorable presentation he gave to atheism as opposed to superstition, and because there were some thoughts in it not to be found in Cicero. Plutarch condemns both superstition and atheism, but nevertheless endows the latter with a certain sturdiness and freedom of thought that make it attractive:

The atheist *thinks* there are no gods, the superstitious man *wishes* there were none; but he believes in them in spite of himself, because he is afraid to die . . . . and would be content with, nay gladly accept Atheist's state of mind, as a state of liberty. But as it is, Atheism has nothing in common with Superstition: for the superstitious man, though by inclination Atheist, is yet far too weak-minded to think about the gods what he wishes to think. And again Atheism is in no way responsible for Superstition—Whereas Superstition has both supplied the cause for Atheism to come into being, and after it is come, furnished it with an excuse.[18]

[18] C. W. King, *Plutarch's Morals* (London, 1889), pp. 272–73.

The implication of this was not lost on the minds of sixteenth-century readers. Cheke translated the treatise into Latin for Henry VIII around 1540 and prefaced it by a long essay, meant no doubt as an antidote to the poison, in which he attacked the atheism of his day. And it must have been Plutarch's treatise Sidney had in mind when he defended the pagan poets for their use of myths and said, "And truly since they had not the light of Christ, did much better in it, than the Philosophers, who shaking off superstition brought in Atheisme."[19]

THE CURRENT OF STOICISM

There was at work in the Renaissance, in addition to the classics of a definitely rationalistic nature such as we have been reviewing, another classical influence of a much more subtle kind. This was Stoicism, a cult which along with Platonism and the other moral systems of antiquity enjoyed a revival in the sixteenth century. The danger of this system to Christianity lay paradoxically not in the antagonism or unlikeness of the two creeds but in their very likeness and in the very ease with which the two appeared to be reconciled. This likeness is partly to be explained by the fact that Christianity itself during its formative period had been strongly tinged with Stoical thought. The apostle Paul, the formulator of the new creed, had been reared in Tarsus, for centuries a center of Hellenistic culture and particularly of Stoicism, and if he himself was not actually one of the Stoics he at least had much in common with them. In fact, Christianity as preached by Paul and Stoicism as taught by Seneca were so nearly identical as far as the virtues and morality were concerned that the Middle Ages could explain the similarity only by supposing that Seneca had been secretly converted by Paul. Moreover, during the first century or two of the new era many other men Stoic by inheritance or training joined themselves to the new creed, not simply as disciples, but to a large extent as teachers also. The influence of these is no doubt to be seen in the fact that the author of the Fourth Gospel bold-

---

[19] *The Defense of Poesie.*

ly placed the Stoic version of the creation at the beginning of
his work. On the whole, there seems to be little doubt that, as
one writer says, Stoicism was one of the "roots" of Christianity.[20]

Now at the beginning of the Renaissance when the classics
began to be read once more as literature, the Humanists soon
discovered that in Seneca and Plutarch there was a system of
morals worthy to be compared with the Christian, and they
saw no reason why this pagan system could not be made auxili-
ary to the Christian. It is very true that Christian morals were
founded on authority and pagan on conscience and reason, but
even in the Middle Ages the church had been willing to call reason and conscience to the aid of revelation and authority. This
attitude was taken up and carried on by such men as Erasmus,
Vives, and Budé, who seem to have wished to bring back pagan
culture with Christianity added, and is very well summarized by
the words of Erasmus, "Remain good Christians but profit by
ancient wisdom." This discovery of another system of morals
worthy to be imitated could have but one effect. It could only
suggest that Christianity had no monopoly on morality. It encouraged a comparison of religions, and it made for the secularization of morality by declaring it to be the province of reason
rather than that of the church.

The popularity of the Stoical writers in the early English
Renaissance is well indicated by the frequency with which their
works were reprinted. In fact, the most striking thing about the
printing of the classics in England during this time is the visible
predilection with which the practical and moral treatises of the
Stoics were printed time after time, long before the great body
of pure literature and the works of the representatives of other
systems had begun to make their appearance. From 1481, when
Caxton printed Cicero's *De amicitia*, on through the sixteenth
century the works of Marcus Aurelius, Dionysius Cato, Cicero,
Epictetus, Plutarch, and Seneca went through dozens of edi-

[20] H. A. Winckler, *Der Stoïcismus eine Wurzel des Christenthums* (Berlin, 1878). See
also E. V. Arnold, *Roman Stoicism* (Cambridge University Press, 1911).

tions. But neither of Homer's works was printed in England before 1580; nothing from Plato, in spite of his popularity, until 1598; nothing from Democritus, Epicurus, or Lucretius before 1600; and, with the single exception of Erasmus' Latin version of *Iphigenia*, none of the Greek dramas until the last decade of the century.

The devil, it would seem, was once more admitted because he came clothed as an angel of light. The opinions of Pliny and Lucretius were easy to refute, at least apparently so, and at any rate their danger was readily evident to all churchmen. But with Stoicism it was otherwise. Closely related to Christianity, urging the same moral virtues, it was advanced by its apologists as an aid to Christianity, and the churchmen, unable to condemn it because of its lofty sentiments, saw little to which they could object. Thus in a way Stoicism actually enjoyed the protection of the church.

That the Humanists saw the tendencies and implications of the system they were reviving is much to be doubted. Certainly they remained loyal to the church and apparently good Christians. Sir Thomas Elyot would properly be one of the last men of his age to be suspected of unbelief, but even in his *Governour* (1531), described by Croft as the earliest treatise on moral philosophy in the language,[21] one of the main influences of Stoicism, the secularization of morals, is already seen to be active. The work shows a complete dissociation of morals and religion, a full moral independence, and in one eloquent passage Elyot goes so far as to give the classics a place superior to the Bible as teachers of virtue.[22]

To summarize: Stoicism made for rationalism because it laicized morals, removed them from the church and placed them in the sphere of reason. Stoicism taught that Fate or Destiny ruled the world, that man's struggles were useless, and thus tended to lessen the moral responsibility of the individual. More

[21] Introd., *The Boke Named the Gouernour*, I, lxiii.
[22] *Ibid.*, p. 371.

important than either of these, it drew men's minds to other religious systems and suggested a comparison not always unfavorable to the non-Christian creeds. From this came inevitably the
observation that all creeds have many points in common and,
in time, the attempt to rediscover and reconstruct the original
belief from which the separate religions were supposed to have
varied. And from this observation and this attempt I think it
not too much to say were derived in a straight line the lofty,
detached skepticism of Montaigne and the deism of Lord Herbert of Cherbury.

II

The Controversy about the Immortality of the Soul

A N OUTGROWTH or development of classical thought of hardly less importance as a source for religious unbelief than the works considered in the previous chapter was the controversy about the immortality of the soul that engaged the attention of so many philosophers and theologians during the course of the sixteenth century. This controversy had originated in the works of Aristotle when they had been made known to Western Europe shortly after the year 1200 and had been long under way before the beginning of the Renaissance. It was then not an outcome of Renaissance thought but rather a continuance of scholasticism, a prolongation of the Middle Ages.

Aristotle, it will be recalled, known to the early Middle Ages only by a few supposititious works, had from about the tenth century on become the special study of the Arabian scholars and philosophers, first at Bagdad and Damascus, and later, when the scene of intellectual activity shifted, in Moorish Spain during the period of religious toleration under the Ommiades. It was in Spain and principally at Cordova that about 1150 the brightest ornaments of the Arabian school appeared, the group composed of Avenpace, Abudacer, Avenzoar, Avicenna, and Averroes. These, in addition to their work in mathematics and medicine, for which they became celebrated throughout Europe, translated with full commentaries a great part of the work of Aristotle into Arabic. But with them the period of rational thought in Spain came to an end. Averroes himself in 1195 found it politic to yield to popular religious prejudice, and after

him Arabian Peripateticism drew to a close and the Moham-
medan world relapsed into darkness.

But the works of these men, and particularly that of Averroes, had by this time begun to penetrate into Christian Europe.
The first introducer of Aristotle with Averroes' commentaries
into Latin seems to have been Michel Scot, whose translation
was made around 1217, and by 1230 sufficient progress had been
made for Roger Bacon to recognize that a new epoch in the
study of Aristotle had dawned. Hermann of Allemand among
others devoted himself to the task of bringing Aristotle from
Arabic into Latin, and by 1250 practically all the works of the
great Peripatetic were available with the commentaries of Averroes. Even this early the Schoolmen were aware that a new enemy of the faith had reared its head. The first scholastic to set
himself the task of refuting Averroes was Guillaume d'Au-
vergne, but after him nearly all the teachers, including Albertus
and St. Thomas, gave some attention to the task.

It was, however, from the first, principally in Northeastern
Italy, at Venice, Padua, Bologna, and Ferrara, that Averroes
exerted his greatest influence. These were the medical centers
of Europe, and it was especially the study of medicine that led
to the reign of Averroes in Italy, for he had been the greatest
physician of his day. Pietro Abano, who may be called the first
Averroist, knew and paid homage to Averroes in 1300. He it
was who began the practice of casting the horoscope of all religions, including the Christian, a practice later taken up by
Cardan and others, and for that impiety the Inquisition ex-
humed and burned his bones. From about 1300 on the Paduan
physicians dedicated themselves to Averroism and from that
time on medical men began to be considered freethinkers. "Physician," "Arabianism," "Averroism," "astrology," and "incredulity" became almost synonymous terms.[1] In Italy before
1500 the principal representatives of the school were Paul of
Venice, Gaetano of Tienne, and Nicoletti Vernias. These kept

[1] Chaucer's doctor was a good Paduan, well grounded in astrology, familiar with
Avicenna and Averroes, and not interested in the Bible.

Averroism alive and often announced opinions of apparent boldness, but after all they were only commentators themselves and
their philosophy was one of words rather than life and thought.
It was not until Pomponazzi that the new era began.

Averroes loomed as such a gigantic figure in the later Middle
Ages and in the Renaissance, exerted so much influence, and was
so frequently combated, that no history of Renaissance thought
that neglects him can be regarded as complete.[2] And his connection with the controversy about the immortality of the soul,
a controversy which he may be said without exaggeration to
have started, makes it necessary here to give some account of
his opinions.[3] The doctrines that the Renaissance called Averroism were not, to be sure, the system of Averroes alone, but of
the entire Spanish-Arabian school to which he belonged. He
was, however, the representative of the system chosen for complete translation into Latin, and his name came to stand for that
of the whole school.

With the rest of the Arabian philosophers and with Aristotle, Averroes believed in the eternity of matter, in a vague,
unknowable God, in law, nature, necessity, reason, and the im-
personality of intelligence. In regard to that question of supreme interest to the Renaissance, the immortality of the soul,
Averroes, although expressing himself with some ambiguity
about details and minor points, left no doubt whatever as to his
main position. It may be said with full certainty that he did not
believe in the personal immortality of the soul. This position
was reached by what we today would call the study of psychology. Averroes followed Aristotle in conceiving of two intellects,
the passive and the active, the first mortal and dying with the
body, the second immortal. But as the active intellect was impersonal, not really a part of the individual but something in

[2] From 1472, the date of the *editio princeps* at Padua, to 1580 his works went through
over a hundred editions in Europe, Venice alone accounting for over fifty of them.

[3] I follow in the main Ernest Renan's excellent work, *Averroès et l'averroïsme* (Paris,
1882), and A. H. Douglas' *Pietro Pomponazzi* (Cambridge University Press, 1910), pp.
3–56.

which he only shared, something that had come to him from the outside world, there was thus no personal immortality. It should be added by way of caution that Averroes did not, as this would seem to imply, believe in the unity of souls, the pantheistic view that all souls are a part of God and consequently immortal. The immortality of the active soul with him seems really to have meant no more than the immortality of the species, the eternal rebirth of humanity and the perpetuity of civilization.

Holding such an opinion as this, Averroes naturally has only aversion for popular myths about the after-life and declares the belief that virtue is a means to happiness in the hereafter to be a dangerous fiction. The man who avoids evil merely because of the hope for a future reward is not really virtuous. In this connection he blames Plato for representing by myths the condition of souls in the future life, and quotes Aristotle in *Generation and Corruption*, who said that a being once corrupted could never completely regain its former condition.

The fascinating horror that such expressions as these had for the Christians of Europe may well be imagined. Averroes himself was no Christian, and in his own person might have been excused for his ridicule of cherished Christian beliefs, but that was not the point at issue. He had interpreted Aristotle to mean these things, and if the Stagirite could be so interpreted the very foundations of Christianity would seem to have begun to rock, and the superstructure might momentarily be expected to collapse.

We have seen that Averroism had been in vogue in Northeastern Italy since about 1300, and that the skepticism about the immortality of the soul that colored the thought of the Paduan school throughout the sixteenth century was thus but a survival of scholasticism. The Renaissance nevertheless had a very positive effect on this phase of medieval thought. Far from discrediting these doubts and setting them aside as it had most of the speculations of the Schoolmen, the Renaissance actually invigorated them, disentangled them from the abstractions of the

Middle Ages, and brought them over into the realm of actuality. Still sheltering themselves behind the medieval doctrine of the twofold truth, the Italian philosophers of the Renaissance nevertheless contrived to impress on their students the fact that the question of immortality was one fraught with the gravest consequences, and thus they started a controversy with which the age never ceased to reverberate.

Chief among those in Italy who added new life to the theories about the soul was the philosopher Pietro Pomponazzi (1462–1525), and his teachings may properly be studied as an epitome of the best thought of the Paduan school on the subject.[4]

The Averroism of Pomponazzi is a point much under dispute, but at any rate it is clear that he did not hold with Averroes that the active soul entered into an impersonal immortality after death. This he denounced as an absurd fiction, and he and his pupils, notably Simon Porta, combated the theory. Pomponazzi's ideal was to return to Aristotle himself and to depend on no commentary, but actually he seems to have embraced the opinion of Alexander of Aphrodisias, a second-century Peripatetic who simply taught that there is no immortality because the ability of the soul to exist apart from the body cannot be demonstrated, and because the soul is dependent on the bodily senses, which perish with the body. He was in line with the Averroists, however, in dividing thought into compartments, reason and faith, and declaring that they are to be kept separate, that it was possible for Pomponazzi the Christian to believe in immortality and for Pomponazzi the philosopher to deny it. But the question of Pomponazzi's Averroism is somewhat academic. The point of interest for us is that he denied immortality about as unequivocally as any man of his day, and other fundamental Christian beliefs as well, and that his teachings, whether directly or by way of France, soon found their way to

4 See Pierre Bayle, *Dictionaire historique et critique* (Rotterdam, 1720); *Encyclopaedia Britannica* (11th ed., 1911); A. H. Douglas, *op. cit.*, pp. 1–3; and John Owen, *Skeptics of the Italian Renaissance* (London, 1893), pp. 184–241.

England, where they formed an important skeptical influence and were many times refuted.

It was in the *Tractatus de immortalitate animae* (1516) that Pomponazzi expressed himself most fully and openly. In this he first takes up and refutes the various systems that had sought to explain the origin and destiny of the soul. St. Thomas and the recent Platonists had given such moral proofs for immortality as the innate need for justice, the universal fear of death, and the universal belief in a life after death. To respond to these arguments Pomponazzi organizes an entirely new system. To work, to suffer with patience, and to die—that is all of life. It has been asked how the duties to his country and to his neighbor may be exacted of a man and if all heroism and disinterestedness will not disappear unless there is a belief in a reward after death. No, says Pomponazzi. Duty is a virtue praised of men, and men had rather die than live in shame. Virtue is its own reward and vice its own punishment. The desire for immortality has been given to men to excite their virtues and restrain their passions. Moreover, the universality of the belief proves nothing, for all men may be deceived as well as one. It is widespread because rulers everywhere have recognized its value in stimulating virtue and restraining vice and have inculcated the belief to make government easier, and for this they are no more to be blamed than a doctor who deceives a child into taking medicine.

As might be expected from his belief about immortality, Pomponazzi was incredulous about other fundamentals of Christianity as well. His position on miracles, for instance, may be briefly noticed. In *De incantationibus*, not published until 1556, thirty years after his death, he takes a realistic attitude toward evidences of supernatural intervention in sublunary affairs, and like Cicero explains miracles on natural grounds. We do not understand the properties of all natural objects; they may have powers that we are not aware of, and miraculous cures are often due to the imagination of the one cured. And all miracles are summarily dealt with as follows: Either they have natural causes, or they are the fruit of the errors of historians, or they are deceptions practiced by priests.

Pomponazzi's position on the whole, and especially in regard to morality, is not unlike Stoicism. It is, to be sure, more extreme than the Stoicism embraced by the serious group of Renaissance thinkers, but the difference is largely one of degree. It is pure paganism, a severe and high system completely opposed to the Christian ideal that had dominated Europe since the fifth century. His works are comparable to no other book before Kant's *Critique of Pure Reason*. It was Pomponazzi and this system that for the next fifty years dominated the thought of the school at Padua, it was with him that the French students found reason for their unbelief, and it was the thought of Pomponazzi and his disciples that the English writers had principally in mind when they leveled their attacks against Italian atheism.

It is unfortunately not possible to trace with any exactness the spread of Paduan religious unbelief to England, for the works of Pomponazzi, Averroes, and Alexander of Aphrodisias were not published in England during the sixteenth century and no famous Paduan, no follower of Pomponazzi or Averroes, that we have any record of, went there to teach. In spite of the fact that from the time of Grocyn and William Latimer English students in ever increasing numbers had been attracted to the Italian centers of learning, England was notoriously slow in the absorption of Italian ideas. From the first the Renaissance in England, under the leadership of More, Colet, Erasmus, and Elyot, had been strongly moral in tone, in contrast to the paganism of France and Italy, and Englishmen had been little disposed to follow the lead of the bolder thinkers of Italy. In addition, the intense English Reformation that quickly ensued engaged the scholars and thinkers, who might otherwise have turned to literature and philosophy, in strictly theological and political controversies, and thus in effect blighted the small beginnings toward intellectual freedom that the Humanists had made. For fifty years the main energies of the English nation were thrown

into this religious quarrel, and it was not until the reign of
Elizabeth was well under way that we find any considerable
number of Englishmen turning to the speculations to which the
French and Italian thinkers had been giving their attention
since the early part of the century.

But it is possible to trace with some definiteness the passage
of Paduan unbelief into France, and since toward the end of the
century the English writers seem to have gained their familiarity
with the thought of Pomponazzi and his group more from the
French than from the Italians themselves, it is necessary to give
some space to this phase of the matter. When the Paduan theories of the soul first began to be discussed in France we do not
know, but the first great Paduan to teach there and to give wide
currency to the theories was the learned Francesco Vicomercato
(1500–1570). Called to France as royal physician by Francis I
in 1530, he was made professor of philosophy in the new College
of France in 1542 and held the position until 1567, when he returned to Italy. Although himself an Aristotelian commentator
who stirred all the questions of the Paduan school, such as the
nature of the soul, the nature of intelligence, the unity of souls,
and immortality, Vicomercato, it should be said, did not follow
Pomponazzi or any other commentator, but ignored them all,
even Plato, and returned to Aristotle himself. He first of all denied Aristotle any place in the Christian system and embraced
his opinion that there is no personal immortality.

With Aristotle he believed the world to be eternal, boldly announced the principle *ex nihilo nil gigni potest*, and thus denied
the Mosaic account of creation. Also with Aristotle he assigned
God a very small place in the universe, relegating him to a remote portion of the heavens and turning the world over to the
operation of natural laws. The name of God appears hardly a
dozen times in his five great works, and that of Jesus Christ
only once, when he is compared to Pierre du Chastel. He was
completely laical, separating faith from reason and substituting
Nature for Providence. Ideas such as his had of course already
been penetrating into France, but his voice came from one of

the highest academic chairs in the kingdom, and he no doubt crystallized the liberal thought of the time (1540–50).

The most important disciple of Vicomercato in France was the physician and scholar Jean Fernel, who in later life wrote only on medicine but whose first book, *De abditis rerum causis* (1548), was a treatise on philosophy. Under the form of a dialogue between Brutus, who is perhaps Fernel himself, and his master, who is clearly Vicomercato, Fernel announces a doctrine of pure materialism, more radical even than that of Vicomercato or Averroes. He proclaims himself a disciple of Alexander and like him believes that the soul is a part of the body and that both are material and mortal. He also argues that matter is eternal and that forms are all that change, and in all respects shows himself a close student of Vicomercato's *De principiis rerum naturalium*. In the latter part of the dialogue Fernel seems to allow Brutus to be convinced of his error, but the change is by no means convincing, and the reader feels strongly that Fernel had stated his own opinions at first.

It will be noticed that the development of Aristotelianism in the Renaissance did not follow any direct line. The fact is that the sixteenth-century Peripatetics, finding Aristotle, Alexander, Averroes, and Pomponazzi all available, chose where their fancy dictated and even struck out on new lines of interpretation for themselves. Nevertheless the Aristotelian strain of thought can always be identified by the preoccupation with the nature and functions of the soul, the discussion of the senses and faculty psychology, and the proofs or disproofs drawn from psychology for the immortality of the soul.

I have not meant to convey the impression here that Aristotle and the Paduans formed the only source of unbelief in France even before 1550. Rabelais and Des Periers (*Cymbalum mundi* [1538]), although living at Lyons, the center of Italian influence, had nothing Italian in their preoccupation or in their arguments. They had perhaps read neither Aristotle nor his commentators but were inheritors of Lucian and Villon. Etienne Dolet and Omer Talon (*Academia* [1548]), were Ciceronians.

Geoffroi Valée, burned in 1572, was perhaps a Stoic and a deist.
Jacques Tahureau (*Dialogues* [written *ca.* 1554]), the precursor
and, according to Pierre Villey,[5] the model of Montaigne, was a
Lucretian. Cardan, however, who had much influence in France,
was concerned with the conventional problems of the Paduans,
announced himself a follower of Averroes, denied, although with
evasions, the immortality of the soul, and repeated that old impiety of casting the horoscope of Christ and the Christian religion.

After 1550 religious unbelief from all sources spread with
great rapidity in France, if we may put any confidence in the
reports of such men as Antoine Fumée, Gentillet, Mornay, Pa-
tard, and La Noue. Libertines, Machiavellians, Epicures, Paduans, and Lucianists increased in number and flourished almost
unchecked, until in 1587 Françoise de la Noue could say that
there were a million Epicures and libertines in France.[6]

Now it seems fairly evident that the English writers of the
last two decades of the century gained their familiarity with irreligious Paduan thought largely from the French unbelievers
and from the French Christian apologists, but there is nevertheless some scattered evidence to show that they were aware much
earlier in the century that the question of the immortality of
the soul was being raised. About 1530 John Rastell published
his *New Boke of Purgatory*, a work divided into three dialogues,
the second of which treats of the immortality of the soul and
refutes directly the Paduan theories. At the beginning Rastell
sets revelation aside and proposes to prove immortality purely
by reason, just as the Paduans had attempted to prove mortality by reason. He then shows that the soul does not depend on
the five senses and that dreams, which he is obliged to argue
that animals do not have, also prove the independence of the
soul from the body. He speaks of the three souls in man, vegetative, sensitive, and intellectual; points to the universal desire
for immortality and to the fact that if there were no life after

[5] *Les sources et l'évolution des essais de Montaigne* (Paris, 1908), p. 37.

[6] *Discours politiques et militaires*, p. 9.

death God would lay himself open to the charge of injustice, justice obviously not being done in this world; and throughout shows himself conversant with the best thought on the subject.

This book of Rastell's is the earliest refutation of the Paduans that I have been able to find in England. The first mention of a definite person in England who denied immortality I have found in the *Fourth Sermon* of Hugh Latimer, preached before Edward VI in 1549. Latimer relates an incident connected with the death of a very wicked man in 1539, and says: "He was a manne the fardest frome the feare of God, that euer I knewe or heard of in Englande . . . . . I haue hearde saye, he was of the opinion that he beleued not the immortalytye of the soule."

The person of course is not named, but from Latimer's method of referring to him it seems that he was well known to the audience, a man of wealth and importance, perhaps an early example of the Italianate Englishman.

In the *Fyfte Sermon*, moreover, in speaking of the present time (1549), Latimer says: "There is a saying that ther be greate maenye in Englande that saye there is no soule, that thyncke it is not eternal, but lyke a dogges soul, that thynke there is neyther heauen nor hell." Two years later Ralph Robinson's translation of More's *Utopia* was published. In the second book More had said one of the main principles of utopian philosophy was the belief in immortality, and opposite this statement Robinson inserted a marginal note saying, "The immortalitie of the soule, whereof these dayes certeine Christianes be in doubte."

Thus it appears that by 1550, in spite of the slowness with which Italian thought made its way to England and the impossibility of tracing the movement in detail, the thought of the Italian philosophers had already become familiar to English writers and large numbers of Englishmen were said to have rejected the belief in the immortality of the soul. In his zeal for the faith Latimer may have overestimated the number of his enemies, but we are probably justified in believing that the report that came to him was not altogether without foundation.

III

Machiavellianism

A CURRENT of thought of Renaissance origin that must be considered in any study of sixteenth-century religious unbelief is Machiavellianism. For if we may trust the statements of both French and English writers of the last half of the century, writers who although contemporary with the phenomena observed and without the historical perspective were nevertheless in a position to know many facts and details that time has obliterated, the works of Machiavelli were the greatest single source of atheism in Western Europe. On this point there was no doubt. Poets, divines, scholars, pamphleteers—all expressed themselves with remarkable unanimity of opinion. Machiavelli was for them the arch-atheist, the devil who had taught men to use religion for political ends, who had corrupted France and brought about St. Bartholomew's Day, who had taught simple Englishmen to be atheists, and who, unless his works were put down or effectively combated, would certainly be the ruin of Christendom. His name, Niccolò ("Old Nick"), at that time became and has ever since remained a synonym for the devil.

The modern reader with these allegations in mind may turn to *The Prince* and *The Discourses*, the works most often inveighed against, and find with some surprise that they are not so entirely subversive to religion and morality as he had been led to expect. This, I think, is to be accounted for by two reasons. In the first place, the moralists and preachers of the sixteenth century, like those of all periods, were inclined to exaggerate the wickedness of their enemies. Strictly speaking, Machiavelli did not teach atheism or even skepticism. He taught a *Real-Politik*, a subordination by a prince of everything, even religion, to his good and 'that of the state. In addition it appears, as I shall show later, that some of the most vehement of Machiavelli's accusers had not actually read his works but had drawn their ideas from other commentators as little likely to be unprejudiced as they themselves. In the second place, the modern reader, with a background in which Hume, Thomas Paine, Huxley, and other outspoken thinkers figure, is likely to underestimate the significance of what Machiavelli does say. There are many chapters in *The Prince* to be sure which have no religious implications and which will bear no interpretation except that of a realistic approach to the problems of statecraft. But a careful reading of chapter xviii, the one most often objected to, will reveal a number of ideas which sixteenth-century churchmen may well be excused for having regarded as dangerous. The last paragraph so well summarizes these ideas that it may be well to quote it:

A Prince therefore is not obliged to have all the fore-mentioned good qualities in reality, but it is necessary he have them in appearance; nay, I will be bold to affirm, that having them actually, and employing them upon all occasions, they are extreamly prejudicial, whereas having them only in appearance, they turn to better accompt; it is honorable to seem mild, and merciful, and courteous, and religious, and sincere, and indeed to be so, provided your mind be so rectified and prepared that you can act quite contrary on occasions. And this must be premised, that a Prince, especially if he come but late to the throne, cannot observe all those things exactly which make men be esteemed virtuous, being oftentimes necessitated for the preservation of his State to do things inhumane, uncharitable, and irreligious; and therefore it is convenient his mind be at his command, and flexible to all the puffs, and variations of his fortune: Not forbearing to be good, whil'st it is in his choice, but knowing how to be evil when there is a necessity. A Prince then is to have particular care that nothing falls from his mouth, but what is full of the five qualities aforesaid, and that to see, and to hear him, he appears all goodness, integrity, humanity, and religion, which last he ought to pretend to more than ordinarily, because more men do judge by the eye, than by the touch, for everybody sees, but few understand; everybody sees how you appear, but few know what in reality you are, and those few dare not oppose the opinion of the multitude who have the Majesty of their Prince to defend them.[1]

[1] *The Works of Nicolas Machiavel,* trans. H. Nevile (London, 1675), p. 223.

There is of course nothing revolutionary here and nothing new. The course of action recommended is one to which shrewd rulers of all times have almost instinctively resorted, and one to which probably all men recognize some inclination in themselves. And herein perhaps lies the explanation of a great many of the expressions of horror that greeted a frank statement of these ideas. Men had tacitly agreed not to recognize these things in themselves and their rulers, to keep them hidden, and to pretend that they did not exist. Machiavelli dragged them out into the light and declared them serviceable.

Then it may be said, and indeed has long been recognized, that Machiavelli did not invent Machiavellianism. Perhaps at no period in English history were rulers more Machiavellian than during the struggle for the crown in the century immediately preceding the one in which the Florentine secretary wrote his works. And Mr. L. A. Weissberger has recently labored to maintain a thesis, which I think will be readily accepted, that for all the talk about Machiavelli in England during the period, Tudor statecraft and policy cannot be shown to have been influenced by him at a single point, and further, where they appear to have been so influenced Machiavellianism was inherent in the nature of the situation.[2] In other words, the machinations of those who directed England's destiny would have differed in no essential particular had Machiavelli never lived or written.

All this can be readily granted, but it must be remembered that the conclusions apply only to statecraft and politics, and that politics, a realm of action, and religion, a realm of thought, are not analogous.[3] Now whether Machiavelli really influenced any considerable number of Englishmen to atheism or not is a question exceedingly difficult to answer. The difficulty is obvious. Some wit has remarked that the devil has never had a fair

[2] "Machiavelli and Tudor England," *Political Science Quarterly*, XLII (1927), 589–607.

[3] H. H. Powers (*Atlantic Monthly*, April, 1923) argues with plausibility that if we were to judge by the *actions* of Europeans we should be at a loss to prove that Christianity itself had had any influence.

show because God has written all the books. And true it is that the devil has rarely had a poorer chance of getting his opinions into print than during the last half of the sixteenth century in England. Consequently at this late date we cannot point to any one man and definitely say that Machiavelli influenced him to unbelief. The contemporaries of such a man were unable to do it with any certainty and even the man himself would probably have had doubts as to the exact source of his incredulity, just as a modern agnostic would perhaps be unable to single out any one piece of writing as responsible for his state of mind.

But one thing is certain. The clergy and other aggressive Christian writers *thought* Machiavelli had influenced large numbers of their countrymen to atheism and acted as if he had, and it may be observed that the clergy, unlike the good women to whom Sidney referred, sick but in faith they could not tell where, have usually been able to diagnose their complaints with a fair degree of accuracy. It may very well have been that members of the profligate Bohemian circles of London, the less steady although intellectually active students of the universities, and especially members of the government espionage service, that is to say, men whose minds were already open to such influences, found in the works of Machiavelli authority and encouragement for the attitude toward which they were already inclined. On the whole I think there is reason to believe that for such men, with the elements of unbelief already in their natures, Machiavelli became a sort of catalytic agent that left them strongly biased against religion and actually disposed to scoff at it.

Like all Italian influences, the current of Machiavellianism made its way to England with comparative slowness. Indeed it was not until the last quarter of the century that the works gained wide currency and seem to have been either read or heard of by everyone who wrote. But these years of popularity were nevertheless preceded by a long period when Machiavelli was known only to a few, mainly to literary adepts, travelers, and scholars. As careful a scholar as Edward Meyer has been misled on this point. "As has been seen," says Meyer, "Machiavelli was utterly unknown in England up to about 1560."[4] The fact is that he was known in England as early as 1528. Cardinal Pole tells us[5] that in 1528 Thomas Cromwell approached him to sound him on the question of the divorce of Henry VIII, and began by asking him what he conceived to be the duties of an adviser to a prince. Pole expressed the correct sentiments about advising a prince to nothing that would compromise his honor, and was surprised when Cromwell replied that these notions were plausible enough when delivered in schools or from the pulpit, but were of little use in the cabinet of kings. Cromwell then expounded his own views that "it became kings to use the specious names of religion, equity, and other virtues, though their designs were not always regulated by them; that true ability lay in managing affairs in such sort as they might obtain their ends, and yet no open failure in religion or probity be observed."

Pole made no reply to "this barefaced impiety" beyond saying he supposed Cromwell had spoken for the sake of argument and not from true sentiments. Cromwell answered that he was not surprised that Pole should feel so, as he had yet had no experience with politics, and ended by offering to lend him a book that would help to clarify his thinking on matters of statecraft. Cromwell did not send the book and Pole believed he had repented opening himself so far. He was able to procure it for himself, however, and, as might have been expected, found it to be a copy of Machiavelli's *Il principe*, "such a performance that, were Satan himself to leave a successor, I do not see by what other maxims he would direct him to reign."

Then if we are to trust Pole's account, and it seems altogether creditable and trustworthy to me, Machiavelli had made his appearance in England in 1528. That he did not remain the possession of one man, that there were others in England not so easily scandalized as Pole, comes to light from a bit of informa-

---

[4] *Machiavelli and the Elizabethan Drama* (Weimar, 1897), p. 38.

[5] In *Apologia ad Carolum V*. Martin Haile (*Life of Reginald Pole* [New York, 1910], pp. 56 ff.) gives full extracts from this work, and on these I have had to depend.

tion in which Pole again figures. In 1540 a certain John Leghe wrote to the Privy Council a report of a conversation he had had with Pole in Rome, and said: "He warned me against reading the story of Nicolo Matchauello, which had already poisoned England and would poison all Christendom, and said he would do all he could to cause it 'to be dystynked and put down hout of remberans.' "[6] By "had already poisoned England" Pole must have meant that Machiavelli's works were widely read and his principles followed there, and Leghe himself lends some verisimilitude to the statement by adding that he intended to get some Italian books when he returned to England, indicating that there was no lack of them there.

It was also some time near the year 1540 that the first attack on Machiavelli that has come down to us made its appearance in England. This was from no less a pen than that of Sir John Cheke. In the essay prefixed to his translation of Plutarch's *Superstition*, already referred to, Cheke censured roundly the atheism of his time, and, leaving that point, passed on to mention another sort of men who make great outward show of religion, even studying divinity, but within are empty of all good works: "And if they are given to alms or fasting, or devotion, they determine not the doing of these things upon any such grounds: But propose to themselves another end of all their actions than God has appointed."[7] The statement, to be sure, is vague, and if it were considered out of its context there might be some reason for regarding it as nothing more than one of the conventional attacks of the clergy on hypocrisy. But when it is remembered that Machiavelli was known to the men of Cheke's circle, and when it is noted that the passage occurs in close connection with an attack on atheism, it seems to me quite likely that it is a reference to Machiavellianism.

Some ten years after these statements by Pole and Cheke two letters were written that link the name of another major figure of English history, William Cecil, with that of Machiavelli. On

[6] *Letters and Papers Foreign and Domestic*, XV (1540), 721.

[7] John Strype, *Life of Sir John Cheke* (London, 1705), p. 251.

December 15, 1551, Sir William Pickering, then at St. Denis, wrote to Cecil that he was having three books bound for him before sending them on to England: "Euclid with the figures in a small volume, and two discourses, one of Machiavelle, the other of Mons. Long. I do not know of any new works."[8] In July of the following year (1552) Sir Richard Morysine also wrote to the future Lord Burleigh, from Villach, where he was ambassador at the court of the Emperor, expressing his indignation that one of his servants had told the Emperor that the ambassador from England was a preacher: "He told all men that I was a preacher and did use to preach every day to my household. I did but read them Bernadine's [Ochine] Prediches for the tongue, and sometimes Machiavel."[9] I suppose Bernadine, the preacher, is mentioned to show how the story originated, although he was read only for the language, and Machiavelli effectively to give it the lie. In both these letters it should be noticed that the name Machiavel is used as if it were perfectly familiar to everyone concerned.

One member of Morysine's household at Villach was probably under no misapprehension as to whether the ambassador was a preacher or not, and no doubt fully understood the purport of the doctrines of Machiavelli which he heard read there. This was Morysine's private secretary, Roger Ascham, the staunch moralist, the man who never lost an opportunity to praise his old master, Sir John Cheke. Having already seen Cheke's attitude toward the atheistical currents of thought in his day, we should have no trouble in predicting the position so devoted a pupil as Ascham would take at a later time. But whatever precepts the younger man received from his master on this point he improved by experience and observation, and the result of his education and mature reflection he expressed in his famous attack on Italian books and influences—an attack that may properly be said to have begun the English reaction against Italianism.

The passage occurs in *The Scholemaster*, written a few months

[8] *Calendar of State Papers, Foreign, 1547–1553*, p. 204.   [9] *Ibid.*, p. 216.

before his death in 1568 and first printed two years later in 1570. As everyone knows, it is a sweeping denunciation of Italian influences in England, of Italian immorality, of the practice of allowing young men to travel in Italy, and especially of the Epicureanism and atheism brought from thence to England. But the point of interest here is that Machiavelli does not escape the general censure. In fact, he is singled out. The Italianate Englishmen, we are told, among other things, "make Christ and his Gospel only serve Civil Policy. Then neither religion cometh amiss to them. In time they be Promoters of both openly; in place again Mockers of both privily."[10] And a few paragraphs farther on, lest there should be any doubt as to whom he had in mind, Machiavelli is mentioned by name, the first time he had been singled out for attack by any writer of importance.

At this time it is necessary to consider a different aspect of the development of Machiavellianism in England, an aspect that will suggest the spread of Paduan thought, which, as we have seen, was introduced into England mainly by way of France. Although it is not likely that Machiavelli was known in France much earlier than in England, it is certain that he was much wider known and read in France and was more influential there around the middle of the century. For instance, at the beginning of Book II of the 1548 French translation of the *Discourses* the statement is made that Machiavelli is better known in France than on the other side of the Alps. And in his Preface to the translation of *The Prince* in 1553 Guillaume Cappel let it be known that he had already heard some vague rumblings of anger against Machiavelli, although he chose not to say that the rumblings were against atheism, with which the Florentine was even then beginning to be charged in France. Moreover, among others, Louis Leroy in his *Consolation à Catherine de Médicis* (1559) proclaimed Machiavelli "un auteur sans conscience et sans religion," and Jerôme Osorio in the third book

---

[10] *The English Works of Roger Ascham*, ed. W. A. Wright (Cambridge University Press, 1904), p. 232.

of his *De nobilitate Christiana* (1571) attacked him with equal violence.

It is not the purpose here, however, to trace in detail the spread of Machiavellianism in France. That has already been done with a wealth of scholarship by Charbonnel, Waille, and Nourrisson. It will be sufficient merely to point out the extent to which this phase of Italian thought affected sixteenth-century France. Indeed, without other evidence a significant commentary on this would be the number of Italians who went to France during the reign of Francis I, men such as Rosso del Rosso, Benvenuto Cellini, Andrea del Sarto, and Leonardo de Vinci in the arts, the two Trivulce in the military profession, and Vicomercato and Da Motta in literature and science, together with literally hundreds of lesser-known figures. The most dangerous of these, said Henri Etienne, were those atheists who, inspired by Machiavelli, counseled Catherine de Medici and prepared the way for St. Bartholomew. Equally significant is the number of editions through which the works of Machiavelli went in France during this period.[11] Two editions of *The Prince* appeared in French translation in 1553, one of which went through five re-editions by 1637. It was again translated into French by Nicolas Lécuper in 1578 and into Latin by N. Strepano in 1599. The *Discourses* first appeared in French in 1548 and were reprinted in 1554, 1559, and 1572. The *Art of War* appeared in 1546 and the *History of Florence* in 1572.

In 1576 as a direct reaction against the rising tide of Machiavellianism in France, the extent of which I have only barely indicated, appeared the most important book ever directed against the Machiavellian current. This was the *Discours sur les moyens de bien gouverner un royaume*, by the Protestant Innocent Gentillet, a work that came habitually to be called *L'anti-Machiavel* or *Contre-Machiavel*. Its importance for us lies in the fact that it immediately became known in England and

---

11 The first edition of *The Prince* that I have been able to discover in England was J. Wolf's Italian edition *Il prencipi* (London, 1584). It was not printed in English translation until 1640 and the complete works not until Nevile's edition of 1675.

was translated in 1577, and especially in the fact that by the spectacular and violent nature of its attacks and accusations it at once became popular and conveyed some knowledge, even though distorted, of Machiavelli to a great many people who had never read his works.

Gentillet organized his assault against the "puant athéist" Machiavel according to a form then popular with theological controversalists, by taking statements or maxims that he regarded as pernicious from various parts of the work and giving a chapter to the refutation of each. This method of course is unfair, for although Gentillet does not actually attribute statements to Machiavelli that he did not make, he boldly misinterprets them and rips them out of a context in which they meant something entirely different. But to be fair was not a part of his plan. His purpose was to cull out everything in Machiavelli that could possibly be regarded as inimical to the Christian religion, and this he did. He wished to fasten the charge of atheism so firmly on Machiavelli that to think of one would be to think of the other, and this also he did. As an example of how he addressed himself to his task the beginning of the refutation of Maxim I may be quoted. The Maxim was: "A Prince above all things ought to wish and desire to be esteemed Devout, although he be not so indeed." Gentillet replied:

This Maxime is a precept, whereby this Atheist *Machiavell* teacheth the prince to be a true contemner of God and of religion, and onely to make a show and a faire countenance outwardly before the world, to be esteemed religious and devout, although he be not. For divine punishment, for such hypocrisie and dissimulation, Machiavel feares not, because he beleeves not there is a God.[12]

The writing of the book was certainly no academic exercise with Gentillet. He was evidently absolutely sincere in the belief that atheism was overwhelming France, and threw his book into the breach in a desperate effort to stem the flood. Time and again he expresses such sentiments as the following:

Yet wee have cause greatly to deplore the miserie and calamitie of the time wherein wee are, which is so infected with Atheists, and contemners of

---

[12] I use the second (1608) edition of Simon Patericke's translation of 1577.

God and all Religion, that even they, which have no religion, are best esteemed, and are called in the court language, People of service; because being fraughted with all impietie and Atheisme, and having well studied their *Machiavel*, which they know upon their fingers, they make no scruple nor conscience at any thing.

In the Preface he had been even more positive in his charges against the courtiers of France:

I doubt not, but many Courtiers, which deale in matters of Estate, and others of their humor, will find it very strange, that I should speake in this sort of their great Doctor *Machiavel*; whose bookes rightly may be called, the French Courtiers *Alcoran*, they have them in so great estimation. . . . .

Moreover, plaine ynough it is, that within these fifteene yeares, *Machiavels* bookes were as familiar and ordinarie in the hands of Courtiers, as the Breviaries in the hands of Curates of parishes.

And, Gentillet concludes, from this familiarity has come all the political trouble of France, civil war, tyranny, and decayed commerce.

This rage for Machiavelli at the court of Catherine de Medici seems not to have passed over into England to any great extent. There was undoubtedly a good deal of Machiavellianism in England by this time, but the Florentine never became an openly avowed favorite at the court of the discreet Elizabeth. It was rather in the reaction to Machiavelli that France influenced England, and in stimulating this reaction Gentillet's book was of paramount importance. With its appearance the references to Machiavelli in English literature rapidly multiplied, and most of these references are of such a nature as to show that it was from Gentillet that the English were drawing their ideas.[13]

There is some reason to believe, moreover, that Gentillet succeeded not only in stimulating the reaction against Machiavelli but also in arousing interest in Machiavelli's works themselves. It was only natural that men with any curiosity at all should desire to read works as evil and as interesting as Gentillet had made these appear, and thus Gentillet had fallen into the error, common to moralists and censors then as now, of becoming the best advertiser of the thing he had meant to destroy.

[13] Edward Meyer noted this fact well when he came across Gentillet's book in the British Museum and called attention to it in his Preface.

By 1579 Machiavelli had become popular at Cambridge, for in that year Harvey wrote:

And I warrant you sum good fellowes amongst us begin nowe to be prettely well acquaynted with a certayne parlous book callid, as I remember me, Il Principe di Niccolo Machiavelli, and I can peradventure name you an odd crew or tooe that ar as cunninge in his Discorsi sopra la prima Deca di Livio, in his Historia Fiorentina, and in his Dialogues della Guerra tooe.[14]

And in the same year in a letter to Spenser: "I beseech you all this while, what news at Cambridge. Tully and Demosthenes nothing so much studied as they were wont. . . . . Machiavel a great man."[15]

But it would be a work of supererogation at this time to follow in detail the spread of Machiavellianism in England and the reaction after the year 1580. Meyer has already done so as far as the drama is concerned, and I shall revert to the matter at the proper place in the following chapters. The directions of the movement have at least been indicated, and although references multiplied in the following years, the lines of the movement seem to have remained about the same. Machiavelli continued to be cursed and reviled and accused of every crime that could be imagined, and in the course of time the charge of Machiavellianism began to be directed at the highest personages in England, Burleigh, Essex, and even Queen Elizabeth not escaping.

Whether gained from Gentillet, or from some other secondary source, or from the works themselves, the knowledge of Machiavelli was indubitably widely spread throughout England at the close of the century. If anyone read his works and remained in doubt as to their religious import, Gentillet and other commentators pointed out to him that the inevitable conclusions of Machiavelli's maxims were nothing less than the negation of all moral principles, religious unbelief, and atheism. Machiavelli was not the only source of religious skepticism in the sixteenth century, perhaps not even the greatest, but that he was an important one the writings of the period leave us no room to doubt.

[14] *Letterbook*, ed. Scott, p. 79.

[15] A. B. Grosart, *The Works of Gabriel Harvey*, I, 68–69.

IV

The Religious Sects and Atheism

A STRONG influence for religious unbelief in England during the last half of the sixteenth century was the warfare of the various religious sects. The Anabaptists, the Unitarians, the Family of Love, the Brownists, the Puritans, and others made their appearance at this time or somewhat before, and all these, as well as the Established Church and the Catholics, boldly claimed to be the sole recipients of divine truth. The vast majority of Englishmen were, of course, arrayed under their various banners, and with an egotism apparently reserved for religious sectaries alone, each sect supposed that God had chosen to reveal the truth to it only and to allow the rest of creation to be misled by the wiles of Satan. But there must nevertheless have been in England a few men not so blinded by prejudice as to see that the struggle of the sects was an indictment of Christianity itself, and there must have been men of a rationalistic turn of mind who found in that struggle additional reasons for their incredulity. Preserved Smith probably says rightly:

> The sight of several churches mutually anathematizing each other's dogmas, criminating and recriminating each other, and giving each other the lie, suggested to the puzzled seeker for truth that possibly all of them were right in their mutual accusations, though each false in its own claims.[1]

There were not lacking writers of the time who called attention to this phase of the matter and who warned England of the opportunity she was giving to atheism by her inability to bring about a settled order of affairs in religion. Thomas Nashe in

[1] *A History of Modern Culture* (New York, 1930), p. 401.

Pierce Penilesse (1592), in addition to pointing to the presence of atheists in England and to the source of their unbelief, let it be known that the religious controversy had allowed their triumph:

> Whence, a number that fetch the Articles of their Beleefe out of Aristotle, and thinke of heauen and hell as the Heathen Philosophers, take occasion to deride our Ecclesiastical State, and all Ceremonies of Deuine worship, as bug-beares scarcrowes, because (like Herodes souldiers) we diuide Christs garments amongst us. . . . . Hence Atheists triumph and reioyce, and talke as prophanely of the Bible, as of Beuis of Hampton.

Five years later as sober a writer as Richard Hooker in *The Laws of Ecclesiastical Polity* rendered the same judgment:

> With our contentions their [the atheists'] irreligious humour is also much strengthened. Nothing pleaseth them better than these manifold oppositions upon the matter of religion, as for that they have hereby the more opportunity to learn on one side how the other may be oppugned, and so to weaken the credit of all unto themselves; as also because of this hot pursuit of lower controversies among men professing religion, and agreeing in the principal foundations thereof, they conceive hope about the higher principles themselves time will cause altercation to grow.[2]

Of the same opinion was Sir Francis Bacon, who in his essay "Of Atheism" (*ca.* 1607) listed as the first cause of atheism division in religion: "The causes of atheism are, division in religion, if they be many; for any one main division addeth zeal to both sides, but many divisions introduce atheism." Similar statements from other writers might be adduced, but these, from a bohemian playwright, a noted divine, and a philosopher, are sufficient to indicate the trend of thought at that time.

But aside from this aspect of the problem, important as it is, there is another and, at least for the sixteenth century, a far more important one. For the Family of Love and other radical sects that came to England from Germany and the Low Countries not only made room for atheism by throwing the ecclesiastical state into disorder, but themselves introduced and held opinions that the divines of the period regarded as little short of atheism. Their beliefs were considered as tending toward the

[2] Book V, Sec. II.

complete negation of Christian principles, toward spiritual anarchy, fatal to both church and state, and in time the conventional method of referring to them came to be Arians, Anabaptists, Familiests, and atheists. In order to throw further light on
the activities of the principal sects in England, the Anabaptists,
the Family of Love, and the Unitarians, it will be profitable to
consider briefly their history and beliefs.[3]

The first group holding Anabaptist doctrines that can be definitely identified appeared at Zurich in 1522 as an extreme wing
of the reforming movement of Zwingli. But Zwingli soon denounced them as too radical, and in 1523 the town council of
Zurich passed a resolution condemning them. In 1525 they were
banished from the town and a sharp persecution began there and
throughout the rest of Switzerland, where by this time they had
begun to spread. By the time of their banishment the sect had
become more decided in their beliefs, rejecting infant baptism
and declaring against the use of force and the bearing of weapons. They had also begun to avow and to some extent to practice the communistic principles for which they were afterward
so often denounced.

Following their banishment from Switzerland, the Anabaptists spread with extraordinary rapidity along the Rhine Valley,
into the Netherlands, and widely throughout Southern Germany, absorbing similar sects and tendencies as they went, and
profiting by the general ferment of ideas that came in the wake
of the Peasant Rebellion of 1525. In Southern and Eastern Germany, in spite of the direst persecutions, torture, exile, death by
fire, the Anabaptists had clung to the doctrine of non-resistance.
But at Munster, in Westphalia, the movement took an entirely
different course. Here in 1529 under the leadership of Roth-
mann and Kipperdollinck the sect had gained some foothold,
building on the disaffection following the outbreak of 1525 and
the subsequent plague and famine, and soon they found them-

---

[3] I follow mainly E. B. Bax, *Rise and Fall of the Anabaptists* (London, 1903); John
Strype, *Annals of the Reformation* (Clarendon Press, 1824); J. W. Allen, *History of
Political Thought in the Sixteenth Century* (New York, 1928); and François Catrou,
Histoire des Anabaptistes (Amsterdam, 1699).

selves in conflict with the authorities. Then followed one of the most extraordinary events of the entire Reformation. The Anabaptists seized and fortified the town, expelled all who refused to accept their faith, and for over a year, 1534–35, successfully resisted a siege of the bishop of the diocese. The city, which was declared to be the New Jerusalem, was organized on communistic principles, a king was chosen, polygamy was made lawful, and a vigorous discipline was maintained—all this by peasants and artisans, for there was not a person of rank in the town and, if a few village schoolmasters be excepted, hardly one of learning. On June 25, 1535, however, the inevitable occurred, and the New Zion went down before the bishop's soldiers. The leaders were tortured and slain and the rest of the rebels expelled from the province, many of them dying of privation and others making their way to the Netherlands and the provinces of South Germany.

The effect of this rebellion was of course to increase the antipathy in which the Anabaptists were already held. They were hated and feared by both ecclesiastical and secular rulers, and the hand of every magistrate in Europe and almost of every person in authority was henceforth vowed to their extermination. Never was a religious movement more completely proletarian in origin. The militancy of the Munster group was of course exceptional and even unique, but that was a fact that rulers could not be expected to know, and besides, as we shall see, almost without exception all groups of the movement were at one in denying any rights of magistrates and in avowing a belief in communism.

It will not be necessary to follow the fortunes of the Continental Anabaptists any further, for already they had begun to penetrate into England. Indeed, although they did not become a serious menace until much later, isolated members of the sect seem to have made their way there very soon after the first appearance of the movement at Zurich, or if not Anabaptists at least heretics of a similar persuasion. Henry d'Anvers in his *Treatise of Baptism*[4] is responsible for the statement that in

4 London, 1674.

1526 seven Anabaptists from Holland were arrested and thrown in prison in England and that two of them were subsequently burned. It was not until 1535, however, that the sect was first mentioned by name in a proclamation. In this year Henry VIII issued an order for bringing in seditious books and denounced

the false opynyon of the Anabaptistes and Sacramentarys that ben lately comen into this realme, wher they lurke secretely in dyverse corners and places myndyng craftely and subtely to provoke and stirr the kings loving subjects to their errors and opynyons.[5]

The proclamation also ordered them to depart the realm on pain of death, and in the same year fourteen who refused to recant were committed to the flames. In 1536 ten others were burned. In 1538 four German Anabaptists were obliged to do penance at St. Paul's Cross and two others were burned at Smithfield.

During the time of Edward and Mary not a great deal is heard of the new sect, but in Bishop Latimer's sermons of 1549 there are occasional references which show that Anabaptism in England had by no means been stamped out. Latimer had heard of one town in which there were five hundred members of the group. The sect continued throughout the early part of Elizabeth's reign in spite of royal proclamations, clerical denunciations, and various forms of persecution, constantly drawing Dutch and German refugees into its ranks and adding to its numbers many English proselytes. Of the year 1575 Strype says:

The anabaptistical sect, that sprang from Germany, was now not uncommon here, especially such as were of the Dutch nation. This year [1575] five of them, condemned for heresy, submitted themselves; namely, Hendric Ter Woort, Gerard Van Byler, Jans Peters, Hans Vanderstrate, and Hemels. In this same year Ter Woort and John Wiemacker were burned at Smithfield, nothwithstanding the earnest intercession of the Dutch congregation. The Privy Council would not spare them for the reason that they would not acknowledge the Council as Christian magistrates.[6]

But by the year 1575 English Anabaptism had begun to take definite shape in the form of a sect calling themselves the Family

---

[5] The entire proclamation is printed by John Strype in his *Memorials of Cranmer*, II, 256, 260.

[6] *Annals*, I, i, 564.

of Love. This sect had been founded by David Georg (Jöris), an Anabaptist of Delft and Basel who had died in 1556, but it was his disciple, Henry Nicholas, who became the apostle Paul of the new movement by organizing his master's beliefs and printing them in numerous books. Nicholas is properly regarded as the founder of the Family in England. In 1574 and 1575 no less than fifteen of his works were translated into English by one Christopher Vittel, or Vitell, of Southwark, and all printed, it seems, at Amsterdam. "About this time or somewhat before," says Strype, "a sect that went by the name of the *family of love* began to be taken notice of. It was derived from Holland; where one H. N. (i.e., Henry Nicolas) was the founder of it." In the same year, 1575, the Family addressed *An Apology* to Parliament professing their innocence of any dangerous opinions and their loyalty to the Queen. Nevertheless Strype adds:

They were bruited forth (and that chiefly by the preachers) for the most detestable sectaries or heretics that ever reigned on the earth; yea, and as people not worthy to live in a commonwealth. That they denied Christ, the Trinity, and the Lord's prayer. That they were libertines, and laid with one another's wives. That they desired to have all men's goods in common. That they accounted whoredom, murder, poisoning, etc., to be no sin. That they denied the resurrection of the flesh, and the immortality of the soul.

The reaction to the Family of Love in England was prompt and vigorous. In 1578 John Rogers published his *Displaying of the Famalie of Love*, in which he traced the Family back to Georg and revealed Nicholas and Vitell as licentious hypocrites. He also proved by summarizing the doctrines of both that the Family and the Anabaptists were but different branches of the same sect and pointed to only two beliefs wherein the Family varied, the denial of the Trinity and the belief that heaven and hell exist only in this world.[7] In the following year appeared two other attacks on the Family, William Wilkinson's *Confutation of Certain Articles Delivered by H. N. unto the Family of Love* and J. Knewstub's *Confutation of Certain Heresies taught by H. N.*, both quite similar to Roger's work except that they

---

[7] This last, it should be noted, was exactly the belief so often attributed to atheists during the period.

dealt in more detail with the practices of the Familiests and opined that they met secretly at night for immoral purposes.

For the next twenty-five or thirty years the Family seems to have enjoyed considerable success with the lower classes in England, to judge from the innumerable references and denunciations they called forth in polemical writings. Bishop John Woolton of Exeter in 1581 discovered a minister in his diocese, Anthony Randall, who held with the Family of Love and promptly unfrocked him. At his trial Randall deposed that the Scriptures, and especially the first few chapters of Genesis, were to be interpreted allegorically, not literally; that paradise was not a real place but was to be understood spiritually or allegorically; and that he could not give his opinion of providence without seeming to speak against the laws of the realm. Bishop Cooper in his *Admonition to the People of England* (1589), a reply to Thomas Cartwright, spoke of the realm being troubled by Papists, "phantasticall spirites of Anabaptistes, of the families of love, and sundry others of the like root," and by an infinite number of Epicures and atheists. In the same year Thomas Nashe in *Martins Months Minde* said, "I meddle not here with the Anabaptists, Famely Lovists, Machiavellists, nor Atheists, ... they are so scattered throughout every forme." Finally may be mentioned Thomas Middleton's play, *The Family of Love* (1607), a poor piece of hack work which I suppose was meant to catch the popular fancy by the title, since members of the sect figure in the play only enough to furnish occasion for some broad humor. The Familiests, of whom several characters are members, are shown as ignorant and degraded people who meet at night without candles for licentious reasons.

It may now be inquired if there is any likelihood that the opinions of the Anabaptists and Family of Lovists could have been regarded as atheistical. It would seem so. In the first place it must have already been observed that the term "atheist" in the sixteenth century had not been restricted to the narrow sense in which it is now used. It included the modern meaning, denial of the existence of God, but a number of other meanings as well, such as the denial of the validity of the Scriptures, deism, agnosticism, Arianism, and sometimes, it would seem, any extreme or radical religious belief. Bacon's care about the definition of terms had led him to note this fact and to remark, "All that impugn a received religion, or superstition, are, by the adverse part, branded with the name of atheists."[8] Moreover, aside from their general fanaticism and irregular practices, which alone would have laid them under suspicion, the Family of Love, as we have seen, held doubts about the Trinity, thought that heaven and hell were only in this world, interpreted the Scriptures allegorically, and were charged with denying the immortality of the soul. Any one of these would have justified the charge of atheism according to the use of the term at that time.

There is indeed actual evidence that these sectaries were called "atheists." Strype reports of Knewstub's *Confutation* that he wrote his book "for the redress of a dangerous enormity, which of late had broken out in this land: he meant this *atheism*, as he called it, brought in by H. N. and his household, who would be called the family of love."[9] A work of a much later date, but not too late, I think, to bear on the subject, is Frederick Cheynell's *Rise, Growth, and Danger of Socinianisme* (1643). The fifth chapter of this work has the title, "Shewes That the Famous Atheists (Anabaptists and Sectaries) So Much Complained Of Have Been Raised or Encouraged by the Doctrines and Practices of the Arminians." Walter, Earl of Essex, in 1576, with a concern for religion that one would have thought incompatible with his character, died lamenting, "There is nothing but infidelity, infidelity, infidelity, atheism, atheism, atheism, no religion, no religion." In view of what we have seen, it is much to be wondered if the Earl did not merely have in mind the Family of Love and other radical sects.

No discussion of the Anabaptists and the Family of Love would be complete unless the relations of these groups to the

---

[8] In his essay "Of Atheism."

[9] *Annals*, II, ii, 302. I have not been able to see Knewstub's work, which is now quite rare, and have had to depend on summaries and extracts.

political theories of the time were considered, for, as it must already have been noticed, it was their political theories as often as not that brought them into conflict with the authorities. The connection of such a discussion with our general subject may not at first seem very close, but I hope to make the connection clear, and to show, by a different method of approach, additional reasons for believing that these groups were considered atheistical.

After the internecine political wars of the fifteenth century, the people of England welcomed the strong, unified rule of the Tudors, and the Tudor sovereigns and their statesmen, ready enough to take advantage of this sentiment, directed their energies toward building up a powerful and undisputed monarchy. This was the keynote of Tudor statecraft. Everything, religion included, was subordinated to this idea. Even the break with Rome and the establishment of a national church, complicated as that movement was by numerous other factors, must in the final analysis be considered but a step in this broad national policy. Formerly only a national sovereign, after the break with Rome Henry VIII had two claims upon the loyalty of his subjects, as Englishmen and as Christians, and from this twofold duty to the sovereign grew the feeling that any religious dissenter, no matter how much he might protest his loyalty, was necessarily disloyal. Religious unity, it was felt, was imperative to national safety. Anyone who failed to conform was a rebel against the king whom God had appointed and therefore against God himself.

And so the constant fear of rebellion that we find expressed in sermons and political tracts throughout the period is easy to explain. In the first place, the uprisings under Jack Cade and Wat Tyler had by no means been forgotten, and the anarchy that had prevailed during the War of the Roses was still fresh in memory. Men would endure almost any tyranny from an absolute ruler rather than open the way for the return of such turbulent times. In the second place, contemporary examples of the horrors of rebellion were not wanting. There were the bloody Peasant Rebellion in Germany in 1525, the Munster uprising of

1535–36, and at a later time the destructive civil wars in France. The adherents of the new monarchy argued with reason that England and all they held dear could not hope to survive the effects of such a rebellion. Finally, the Tudors and their statesmen could never forget that England was "round about environed" with enemies. Scotland, France, Spain, and the papacy hovered always in the offing, ready at the slightest opportunity to strike a deadly blow, and ready to make such an opportunity by any possible means. Under such circumstances it was recognized that a rebellion that could not be promptly suppressed would be nothing short of suicidal for England. And thus the reasons why Cromwell dotted the landscape with gibbets and the reasons why Elizabeth, usually so hesitant to shed blood, put down the northern rebellion with the ruthlessness of an oriental despot are easy to understand. Religion may have been one factor, but it was only one. The main reason was Tudor statecraft.

Now the rebels chiefly feared and the ones against whom most of the attacks were directed were of course the papists, but, as we have already seen, the Anabaptists and their different offshoots entertained political opinions that caused them to be held in the greatest antipathy and that were responsible for more than one of them being led to the stake. They avowed communism; they refused to take an oath; they held that resistance was evil and therefore refused to bear arms; and, worst of all, they denied any rights, spiritual or temporal, to magistrates. For a number of reasons, perhaps partly because of the rather weak claim of the Tudors to the throne and because of the question of Elizabeth's illegitimacy, the matter of mere recognition of rights was of far more importance in the Tudor period than it would be now, and anyone who failed to recognize the rights of magistrates was regarded as extremely dangerous to the state, a potential rebel if not an actual one. That the Anabaptists were actual rebels in England there is almost no evidence to show, and they frequently protested their innocence and loyalty. Yet they were general trouble-makers and disturbers of tranquillity, and the Munster Rebellion must have been constantly in the minds of magistrates as an example of what might be expected from them if they gained much headway in England.

Now it is known to be a fact that in the thought of the sixteenth century there was a close connection between sedition and atheism. So far as I am aware there is no actual evidence to show that rebellion in itself was regarded as atheism or that it was ever so called, but it must not be forgotten that the people of England in their national fervor and in their zeal for a strong monarchy had elevated their rulers to an extremely high position. The king was God's vicar on earth and, more than that, he was the head of God's church. Rebellion against the king, then, as it was often said, was rebellion against God, and, having said so much, a logical mind would take the next step and say that denial of the rights of the sovereign was tantamount to a denial of the existence of God. This last step seems not to have been made, at least not in writing, but the writers are constantly approaching it and almost taking it, and in their minds they may actually, if perhaps unconsciously, have done so. It will be recalled in this connection that the accusations of atheism made against Kyd and Marlowe followed a charge of sedition. Marlowe and his associates in the espionage service were seditious atheists. Even more to the point is the fact that Thomas Lodge in *Wits Miserie and the Worlds Madnesse* (1595) treats sedition immediately after atheism, thus showing how closely the two were associated in his mind.

Aside from this argument, which I grant to be somewhat tenuous and far from conclusive, is the undeniable fact that rebellion was regarded as one of the most heinous of all sins. Throughout the century all preachers and political writers who have left any record of their thoughts, even including the Puritans near the end of the period, unite in an unqualified denunciation of the sin of rebellion. True enough this was an argument of counsel. Rebellion menaced their interests, and it was a great sin because the preachers found it expedient to consider it so. Nevertheless,

for whatever reason, they did consider it so, and this sin of rebellion added to the other sins the Anabaptists and the Family
of Love were said to be committing probably increased to a
considerable extent the likelihood of those groups being called
atheists.

The beginnings of Unitarianism in England are almost impossible to trace with any definiteness, but it is certain that some
form of the heresy was known there quite early in the sixteenth
century. It is in fact to the works of Erasmus that we must go
for the first hints of the movement. In his annotations and in
the Preface to the *Works of St. Hilary* we find utterances tending
to destroy the chief scriptural arguments for the Trinity. Particularly is this so in his note upon I John 5:7, a verse that he
omitted on the authority of the Fathers and the oldest manu-
scripts.[10] He explains as follows:

> But some will say that this verse is an effective weapon against the Arians.
> Very true. But the moment it is proved that the reading did not exist of old,
> either among the Greeks or among the Latins, this weapon is no longer worth
> anything. . . . . Far better it is to employ our pious studies in endeavouring
> to resemble God, than in indiscreet discussions with a view to ascertaining
> wherein the Son is distinguished from the Father, and wherein the Holy
> Ghost differs from the other two.

Of course Erasmus with his pliable temper was able to abandon
this position with celerity when he was called in question. "All
my studies, in innumerable places," he defends himself by saying, "clearly proclaim agreement with the definition of the
Trinity handed down by the Catholic Church." Again he makes
his attitude toward the church even clearer by saying, "The
Church has so much authority in my eyes, that I would sub-
scribe to Arianism and to Pelagianism, if these doctrines were
approved by the Church." Matters of belief were not important to Erasmus, but there is a probability that he inclined toward Arianism, and it is certain that by his philological exegesis
he supplied weapons to the adversaries of the Trinity, and par-

[10] According to the King James Version, "For there are three that bear record in
heaven, the Father, the Word, and the Holy Ghost: and these three are one."

ticularly to the Anabaptists in the Low Countries. It is perhaps not without significance that Erasmus showed a strong spirit of tolerance toward these people and pleaded their cause against the magistrates of Zurich.

Another international scholar of the time who contributed much to the development of Unitarianism, but who, unlike Erasmus, had the courage of his convictions and suffered martyrdom, was Michael Servetus.[11] The heart of Servetus' teachings on the subject of the Trinity is the denial that God is three persons. His position may be fairly summed up in one passage from *De Trinitatis erroribus:*

> The only Trinity is a trinity of manifestations or modes of action, not of persons, and that trinity will cease in the eternal world. The Word, when God utters it, is *God himself speaking*, and since the Word was man, we understand by it Christ himself, who is the Word of God. There is no other Person of God but Christ, and all theories of the Divine nature, apart from the Word, are blasphemies against Christ.

Thus his Unitarianism was not of a very radical order, only the belief that Christ and the Holy Ghost were manifestations of the unified God, but it was sufficiently advanced for the time and required his death. Two other points of his theology deserve mention. He taught, in contrast to Melanchthon, that salvation can be grasped here and now and is not something to be expected in the future, and he rejected infant baptism with great scorn and vehemence, pronouncing it little more than magic or sorcery against the superstition of a birth curse.

The points of concurrence that must have been noticed between the theology of Erasmus and Servetus and that of the Anabaptists were not merely the result of coincidence, for the Anabaptists, at least at the beginning, held a number of anti-Trinitarian dogmas. Together with the Unitarians they placed the word of God above human tradition, as represented by the papacy, and contemplated a radical reform of the church. They believed that what makes a real Christian is his life and not his dogma, and thus that real Christian faith dates only from con-

---

[11] When fleeing from persecution at Lyons and trying to make his way to Italy, he was apprehended by Calvin at Geneva in 1553 and burned to death.

version, and in common with the Unitarians most of the Anabaptists denied the orthodox dogma of the incarnation. One of
the most active Anabaptists, David Georg, the founder of the
Family of Love, left no doubt as to his opinion on the Trinity.
"There is but one God," said he, "sole and indivisible, and it is
contrary to the operation of God throughout creation to admit
a God in three persons, or that the three make but one, as
taught in the Athanasian Creed."[12] And his disciple, Henry
Nicholas, who brought the Family to England, followed Georg
closely in his denial of the Trinity ontological. There were of
course other sources for Unitarian thought in England than the
Anabaptists, and especially toward the end of the century when
the influence of Fausto Sozzini began to be felt, but it seems
clear that in the time of the Reformation it was the Anabaptists
who brought the doctrine to England and who were its first active advocates.

The first stir about Unitarianism in England seems to have
occurred about the years 1548–51, during which time several
Unitarian heretics were ferreted out to the accompaniment of
much ecclesiastical thunder and carried to the stake. In 1549
Bishop John Hooper complained in a letter to Bullinger that the
Anabaptists were giving much trouble in his diocese and that
they held strange opinions of the incarnation of Christ, denying
that he was born of the Virgin Mary. And he adds the lament:

Alas, the ancient heresies, dead and buried, are revived among us and new
ones come to notice every day. Thus there are some libertins sufficiently bold
in their statements not only to deny that Christ was the Messiah and the
Savior of the world, but also to declare that he was a miserable companion
and the seducer of the world.[13]

Two other events make the year 1549 notable in the history
of the Unitarian heresy. One was the burning of Joan of Kent,
by Cranmer's order, for her fantastic ideas of the incarnation;
the other, the appearance of John Proctor's work, *The Fal of*

---

[12] As quoted by Gaston Bonet-Maury in *Des origines du christianisme unitaire chez
les anglais* (Paris, 1881), pp. 60–61.

[13] *Zurich Letters* (3d ser.), Letter 33.

the Late Arrian, the first book printed in England devoted entirely to the refutation of Unitarianism. The plan of Proctor's book was simple. There had fallen into his hands a document addressed to a bishop or archbishop by someone suspected of the heresy and apparently in prison, and this work, a defense of Unitarianism, Proctor took up and refuted section by section, citing scripture and adding many pious reflections not very apropos to the argument. From the Preface we learn that the man whose fall he was celebrating was not the only Arian in England, for the heresy was "presentlye riefe amongeste the people" and there were many who feared not "impiously to auouche, teache and affirme, that Jesus Christ is not true god, but a mere creature, a passable man only."

In 1579 a Dutchman, Georg van Paris, who denied Christ to be true God, came to a like end with Joan of Kent and was burned at the stake. In the same year Martin Microen, a French preacher to the Church of the Strangers, founded by Edward VI, wrote to Bullinger saying:

The principal adversaries of the divinity of Jesus Christ are the Arians, who are shaking our church with more violence than ever in denying the conception of Christ by the Virgin. Their principal argument concerns the unity of God. They maintain that the name of the Trinity is a new invention of which no mention is made in any passage of scripture.[14]

Beginning in 1579 there was a series of burnings at Norwich for Unitarianism. A plow-wright of Hetherset, Matthew Hamont or Hammond, was tried by the Bishop of Norwich "for that he denied Christ" and burned May 20, 1579. He alleged among other things:

That Christe is not God, nor the Savior of the world, but a meere man, a sinfull man, and an abhominable idoll.

That al they that worshippe him are abhominable Idolaters; And that Christe did not rise agayne from death to life by the power of the Godhead, neither, that hee did ascende into Heaven.

That the Holy Ghoste is not God, neither that there is any suche holy Ghoste.

That Baptisme is not necessarie in the churche of God.[15]

[14] *Ibid.*, Letter 265.   [15] Stow, *Annals of England* (1615), p. 695.

In 1583 John Lewes and in 1587 Peter Cole, an Ipswich tanner, were also burned at Norwich for "denying the Godhead of Christ, and holding other detestable heresies." The most famous of this group, however, was the Cambridge Fellow, Francis Kett. He had left the university in 1580 and seems to have been orthodox enough up until 1585, when he returned to his home in Norwich. Here he became infected with some form of the Arian heresy and soon found himself in the hands of the Bishop of Norwich, by whom he was promptly tried and burned in 1589. The principal heresies to which Kett confessed during his trial were as follows:

> That Christ was not High Priest until his Assention into Heaven.
> That the Holie Ghost is not god, but an Holy spirite.
> That there is no such persone and that God is no person.
> That Christ is only man and synfull as other men are.
> That there is no hell until that tyme shall come, specified to before.
> That no children ought to be baptized before their full age and to know what they should beleave.[16]

There is, to be sure, much in the confessions of Kett and Hamond for which Unitarianism cannot be held responsible, fanaticism with Kett and apparently a rather advanced incredulity with Hamond, but from the general tone of the confessions and from the main points it seems likely that at the beginning their unbelief had been of Unitarian origin.

No long argument is needed to prove that Arianism was considered and called "atheism." For whether merely denying the incarnation, or holding that Christ was not an equal member of the Trinity, or pointing to his physical attributes as evidence that he was only a man, all Arians were at one in denying that he was fully a divinity, that he was true God, and any such opinion on the face of it was atheism in the sixteenth century.[17] No better evidence can be brought forward that this is so than the charge of atheism against Thomas Kyd, a charge made on the sole ground that he had in his possession a paper that de-

[16] Printed by Grosart in *Life and Works of Robert Greene*, I, 259.

[17] Indeed, members of the more evangelical churches may still be heard to say that a Unitarian is little better than an atheist.

fended Unitarian doctrines. The abject terror into which Kyd was thrown and his frantic denials of any such opinions and even of ownership of the paper show further that the lesson of the Norwich burnings had been learned to the fullest. To avow Unitarianism or atheism was merely to sign one's own death warrant.

Half a century later, in 1643, Frederick Cheynell rendered a judgment which shows that neither Unitarianism nor its adversaries had undergone any significant change during the interval. Cheynell begins chapter v of his *Rise, Growth and Danger of Socinianisme* by saying:

There hath been a great complaint of late that men are turned Atheists, and surely not without cause, but let us sadly inquire into the reason. The Socinians doe deny Christ to be God to the glory of God the Father, as they use to say, and I beleeve God the Father hath taken it so unkindly at their hands, that he hath given them over to that cursed Atheisme which reignes in the heart of every man by nature.

Cheynell adds further that the Socinians, as the Unitarians were then called, set open wide gaps to other kinds of atheism, such as libertinism, and that by calling in question the very fundamentals of the Christian faith they laid all other points open to doubt.

Cheynell is of course too late to have much importance for sixteenth-century Unitarianism, but his work is interesting as showing the later developments of certain principles the Unitarians had held from the first. In one passage in particular he touches upon the implications of one of their principles that was to become of increasing importance during the following century. I refer to the principle of reason:

The Socinians, Cheynell says, lay the principle of reason as their foundation, and keep so close to it that they reject the weightiest Articles of the Christian faith, because Reason cannot discover them to be true by her own light, that is reason (*ante Spiritus sancti illustrationem*) before the illumination of the Holy Ghost, as they explain themselves. . . . . Reason by its own light did discover unto them that the good and great God had prepared eternall happiness for our immortall soules: if this then be enough (as the Socinians say it is) to receive all things as Principles of Religion which Reason by her own light can discover to be true . . . . then the Philosophers, especially the Platonists, were in an happy condition, and it will be lawfull for a man to cry out aloud, *Sit anima mea cum Philosophis*, and he shall never be thought an Atheist. . . . . Let us then Canonize the Heathen for Saints, and put Hermes, Phocylides, Pythagoras, Socrates, Plato, Plotinus, Cicero, Zorcaster, Iamblichus, Epictetus, Simplicius into our Rubrike, and let not Aristotle, Alexander, or Averroes be left out.

Thinking he was pushing the arguments of the Socinians to the utmost limits of absurdity, Cheynell really delivered a fairly accurate prophecy of what was to take place in the development of philosophical thought during the next hundred years. It was exactly this rationalistic tendency that became so characteristic of the late seventeenth and eighteenth centuries. Now eighteenth-century deism was a movement of the greatest complexity, and any simple explanation of its origin, no matter how plausible, ought to be regarded with suspicion. Deism was a stream with many sources. Nevertheless, the Socinians with their insistency on the principle of reason seem to me to have become, if not its main source, at least one of its more important tributaries.

V

The Reaction to Atheism (1530-60)
Rastell, Cheke, Latimer, Hutchinson, Veron

THE inquiry into religious unbelief in the English Renaissance has thus far been, and in the nature of the case must continue to be, founded upon the reaction to that unbelief rather than upon the thing itself. The reason for this is the perfectly obvious one that the information cannot be gleaned from any other source. The numerous refutations of atheism and other forms of unbelief that continued to appear from 1530 on are, it must be supposed, the strongest sort of presumptive evidence that there were men in England who held such opinions, for upon any other assumption we should be forced to conclude that the clergy and numbers of devout laymen had abandoned common sense and united for an assault on windmills. Such a thing is most improbable. The English churchmen of the Reformation were one of the most sternly practical groups of which ecclesiastical history affords any record. They stood surrounded by active and powerful enemies of a most substantial kind, and they never showed the slightest disposition to conjure up imaginary foes or to whet their swords for a warfare on chimeras.

But to be convinced that there were religious freethinkers in England and to be able to identify them are not the same. The difficulties in the way of pointing them out are readily intelligible. Common prudence would require that the man who doubted the dogmas of the church should not jeopardize his life by putting his doubts in writing and that he should not reveal himself except to his closest friends. If news of his opinions came to the authorities he would of course deny everything, unless he happened to be a religious dissenter, in which case he might feel obliged to tell the truth and suffer for the sake of his religion. If he had been led into unbelief by reading the classics, by studying the works of Machiavelli, or by familiarity with the current doubts about the immortality of the soul, he might give vent to his doubts to tavern companions or in the freedom of after-dinner discussion among men of his own temper. And thus in the course of time it might be rumored about that a certain person was an atheist, but there would be nothing but inadmissible hearsay evidence and consequently no names mentioned in the records.

Notwithstanding the difficulties in the way of naming and reviewing the beliefs of sixteenth-century freethinkers, however, no inconsiderable amount of information about them may be gathered from a study of the attacks directed against them. Working within certain definite limits, I think we may yet hope to throw some light on the history and development of a phase of English thought in the Renaissance that has thus far received only the most cursory attention from historians and that as a result has remained in almost total obscurity. If this can be done, it seems to me that the mere identifying of people who were not able to leave any record of their thoughts, which would amount to little more than the unearthing of meaningless names, becomes a matter of relative unimportance.

The preceding chapters, devoted to showing the sources for religious unbelief in the Renaissance, have shown also that whatever free thought was in England was almost entirely of foreign origin. The Renaissance, especially in its early stages, was for England a time of importation and assimilation of ideas and not one of great originality. It has likewise been mentioned in the preceding chapters, although not with the emphasis that the matter will later receive, that the various English works which refute atheism are often based on or inspired by similar refutations which first appeared on the Continent. Then even the reaction to atheism cannot be said to be English in origin, and from this it follows that atheism in England and the reaction to it were not necessarily very intimately connected. Sometimes they were, as we shall later see, but not always. The point to be made is that the English attack on atheism, moving somewhat apart from and independent of religious unbelief in England, is in itself a phenomenon of some interest and one that we could study with profit, even if we were obliged to disbelieve in the local existence of the thing at which it purported to be aimed. Hence the purpose of the following chapters will be twofold: first, to study the English attack on free thought for the light it will throw on the nature and extent of that free thought; and, second, to study the attacks as a separate movement, to note their relations to each other, their sources, their conventional features, to review their main arguments, and in general to consider them as a distinct body of literature.

The point just under observation, that is, the appearance of a reaction in the Continental tradition apparently before there was anything in England to account for it, is well exemplified by a work already discussed, the first of the kind that has come to my attention. This is John Rastell's *New Boke of Purgatory*, written in 1530 or shortly before, and divided into three dialogues, the first treating of the existence of God, the second of the immortality of the soul, and the third of purgatory. The second of these is the one that most nearly touches our subject, for in it Rastell undertakes to prove by purely natural reasons that the soul is immortal. The reasons turn out to be the conventional ones so often met with in similar works throughout the period, and can really be summed up as evidences that the soul is capable of a separate existence from the body. The arguments here are mainly that the soul leaves the body during dreams and that it can know things without the aid of the senses, a sort of transcendentalism. So it is clear that the chapter is directly in the peripatetic tradition, a part of the great controversy about immortality that had been carried on ever since Aristotle had been introduced to the Western world by the Arabs around the year 1200.

Rastell's work is of especial interest because of its early date.

It shows that by 1530 the thought of Pomponazzi and his disciples, who had given the controversy new life at the Renaissance, was already beginning to penetrate into England, and that this thought was regarded as of sufficient importance to demand a reasoned reply. True enough, Rastell seems never to have heard of Pomponazzi or of any of the other skeptical commentators and points to no skeptics in England, but he had read Aristotle's *De anima* and knew on what grounds the battle was being waged. Indeed, his familiarity with the conventional arguments on both sides and the glibness with which he states his conclusions seem to indicate that even he was dealing with well-known material. At any rate, this work effectually sets aside the theory formerly held that the disputations concerning immortality were first introduced into England by the writings of such men as Mornay in the time of Sidney. They had been known all along, and had it not been for the intensity of the English Reformation, in which minor controversies were lots sight of, evidences of the struggle might be as easy to trace as they are in France during the same period.

Two other works already referred to are Cheke's essay *On Superstition*, around 1540, and Bishop Latimer's sermons of 1549, with their references to those who are denying immortality. Cheke seems to have been the first writer in England who used the word "atheist," a term he applied to certain groups who denied providence and cared not if there were a God in the world, probably Lucretians or Lucianists, and he delivered what I consider to be the first formal attack against Machiavellianism.

I think we may say, then, that at least by 1549 the lines of the battle against atheism are already pretty well drawn. Paduan thought is certainly present and is recognized as a great danger, Machiavellianism is rapidly becoming a serious menace to the faith, and the Lucretians and Lucianists have appeared. We have already seen that the Anabaptists with their Pelagian and Unitarian opinions became important quite early in the century and that Unitarianism itself called forth a vigorous reply in 1549.

During the subsequent decades, unbelief from all these sources, and probably from others as well, spread more widely and the attacks on it became more frequent and more intense, but practically the same ground continued to be fought over and the lines of the battle remained almost unchanged throughout the rest of the century.

An element of variety is lent to the struggle by Roger Hutchinson, who in his *Image of God or Layman's Book* (1550) discovered a new source of irreligion in the current practice of astrology. This was a study that had been extremely popular throughout the Middle Ages but that appears to have declined somewhat at the beginning of the Renaissance. Around 1550 for some reason there was a revival of interest in the subject, not only among the classes which have been its principal support through the ages, the ignorant and superstitious, but curiously enough among some of the most learned men in England and especially, it seems, among the nobility. Writing about 1550, Lawrence Humphrey in his *De nobilitate* exhorted the nobility to a study of the sciences but observed that astrology was "so snatched at, so beloved, and even devoured by most Persons of Honour and Worship, that they needed no Inticement to this, but a Bridle rather. . . . . And that many had so trusted to this, that they almost distrusted God."[1]

It was this tendency to distrust God that had alarmed Hutchinson, for he had seen, clearer than most men of his time, the full implication of a belief in astrology. He had seen that the influence of the stars, so much studied by Christians, and the fate or destiny of the Stoics were practically the same thing, and he had recognized that a belief in such an influence was tantamount to a denial of God's direct providence over his creatures. In one place he states the issue very concisely:

Others grant God to be the maker of all things: but they suppose that, as the shipwright, when he hath made the ship, leaveth it to the mariners, and meddleth no more therewith; and as the carpenter leaveth the house that he hath made; even so God, after he had formed all things, left all his creatures

[1] Quoted by Strype, *Life of Cheke*, p. 138.

to their own governance, or to the governance of the stars; not ruling the world after his providence, but living in ease and quietness, as the Stoics, Epicures, and divers astrologers.[2]

The entire chapter in which this occurs is written principally against the Epicures, Stoics, and others who deny God's providence, but usually with immediate reference to the astrologers, since they were for Hutchinson the most notorious of the modern deniers of providence.

But groups that occasioned Hutchinson even more anxiety were the English Sadducees, as he calls them, and the libertines, both of whom he refutes at some length. According to Hutchinson's treatment, it is hard to differentiate between these groups, as he usually mentions them together and attributes about the same opinions to them. But it is clear that his Sadducees owed nothing to the Jewish sect and that his libertines were not necessarily men of loose moral principles. Both held, according to Hutchinson, that angels were not substances but inspirations, affections, and qualities, good angels the godly notions that God inspires in us, and evil angels the beastly affections and evil thoughts that come of the flesh, and both denied heaven and hell and the resurrection, saying that these were to be interpreted allegorically. "But our Sadducees grant the resurrection," says Hutchinson ironically. "They say, 'We must rise from sin, if we will come to heaven, which is a merry and joyful conscience.' " He of course protests that the resurrection from sin is but a type of the other resurrection and that heaven and hell are both real places.

In this same chapter, the twenty-fourth, Hutchinson becomes somewhat more outspoken toward the end and practically accuses the Sadducees of being atheists, "I think such have already said in their hearts, 'There is no God'; or that they may easily be brought thereunto," and refers also to the likelihood of their disturbing the commonwealth and their love of discussion. From these things and from their allegorical interpretations of the scripture it seems almost certain that Hutchinson's Sad-

[2] *Works of Roger Hutchinson* ("Parker Society Reprints"), p. 69.

ducees and libertines were nothing more than one of the radical religious sects closely related to the Anabaptists and the Family of Love. Their opinions, in fact, are almost precisely those attributed by Strype to a group in England called the Family of the Mount.[3]

The next writer we find who applied himself to a refutation of atheism was the learned French preacher John Veron, who first came to England as pastor of the French congregation in London during the time of Edward VI. About the time of Elizabeth's accession he published his *Frutefull Treatise of Predestination and Providence, against the Swynishe Gruntings of the Epicures and Atheystes of Oure Time*, bearing the subtitle, *An Aunswer Made to All the Vayne and Blasphemous Obiections That the Epicures and Anabaptistes of Oure Time Can Make*. This is a promising title and we should expect the work to supply us with much information and with important details, but we are disappointed to find that Veron did not have much to add to what his predecessors had already said. It is the first part of his title, the question of predestination, that principally engages his attention, and that mostly in a purely theological way, the atheists and Epicures receiving only incidental reference.

In only one place am I able to see any originality in Veron. This is when he undertakes to reply to the suggestion that predestination ought not to be discussed, since worldly men are prone to scoff at it:

Prophane and carnall menne wyll take no lesse occasion too blaspheme . . . . when they shall understand that it is but a lyttle more than fyue thousande yeares a goo sens the worlde was made. Wyll they not bothe scornefullye and also blasphemouslye aske what God dyd all that whyle affore? And whye hys power and vertue was idle and unoccupyed so longe? What shall ye be able to saye or wrytte, but that they wyll take occasion oppon it, too blaspheme God and hys work?[4]

---

[3] *Annals*, I, i, 563. "The sectaries of the family of the mount held all things common and lived in contemplation altogether; denying all prayers and the resurrection of the body. They questioned, whether there were an heaven or an hell, but what is in this life. . . . . As heaven was, when they do laugh and are merry; and hell, when they are in sorrow, grief, or pain. And lastly, they believed that all things came by nature."

[4] Fols. 6–7.

This scoffing at the idea of the world's being only five thousand years old and raising questions about the creation may have been caused by one of two things. The new conception of the universe and man's place in it that was gradually resulting from the geographical and astronomical discoveries, together with the discoveries of great bodies of savage people of whom the Bible had made no mention, may this early have begun to cause some doubt as to the truth of biblical cosmology. On the other hand, these doubts may have originated in the conflict between the cosmologies of Aristotle and Epicurus and the biblical account of creation. Aristotle had implied the eternity of the world and many of his commentators, notably Averroes, had affirmed it. But it must be acknowledged that the application of Veron's remarks to his own time is made somewhat difficult by his reference to those who ask what God did before he created the world, for this is the question that Augustine in his *Confessions* said had often been asked. Augustine would not reply, as some had, that during that time God had made hell for inquisitive fools, but merely answered that such things were beyond human knowledge.

VI

The Reaction (1560-90)
Ascham, Woolton, Lyly, Sidney, Harvey

WITH the attack on immorality and atheism in Roger Ascham's *Scholemaster* (1563–68) we definitely enter into a new era for our subject, an era in which the vagueness that had characterized the earlier attacks, while not entirely disappearing, at least decreases considerably, and in which certain causes for unbelief, before only hinted at, come to be clearly recognized and stated. With Ascham the Italianate gentleman enters into the discussion, and Italy itself begins to be considered not the source of learning and culture it had been for the last hundred years or more, but a center of vice, depravity, and atheism. And with Ascham there also enters the belief that romances and lascivious stories, particularly those of Italian origin, are corrupting the youth of the land and enticing them into a scorn of religion. Finally, we have with Ascham, as we have already observed, the first mention of the name Machiavelli in a work of this sort.

The author of the *Scholemaster* was led into his attack on Italian atheism by his careful study of the education of a young man, for the question naturally arose as to whether or not the youth should be allowed to travel into Italy. But he soon passes to a general denunciation of Italian romances, which now that they are being translated into English are doing more harm than *Morte d'Arthur* had ever done, and to a stirring rebuke of the Italianate Englishman. "Thies men," he says, "*abhominabiles facti in studijs suis*, thinke verily, and singe gladlie the verse before, *Dixit insipiens in Corde suo, non est Deus*."[1] And next

---

[1] The reference is to Ps. 14:1, "The fool hath said in his heart, There is no God."

he proceeds to show exactly into what temper of mind these
foolish men had been led by their too great love for Italian
authors:

Than they haue in more reuerence, the triumphs of Petrarche: than the
Genesis of Moses: They make more accounte of Tullies offices than S. Paules
epistles: of a tale in Bocace than a storie of the Bible. Than they counte as
Fables, the holie misteries of Christian Religion. They make Christ and his
Gospell onlie serue Ciuill pollicie. In tyme they be Promoters of both openlie:
in place againe mockers of both priuilie.[2]

And he adds a moment later: "They that do read, with indifferent iudgement, *Pygius* and *Machiauel,* two indifferent Patri-
arches of thies two Religions, do know full well that I say
trewe."

What information relative to our subject may we deduce
from Ascham's remarks? In the first place, we may say that he
was speaking of a court group, of young noblemen who had
traveled in Italy and returned to enter the service of Elizabeth.
It should be added that Ascham had every opportunity to be
familiar with this group, for he had been connected with the
court or associated with courtiers almost constantly since he
had left Cambridge. But what particular phase of Italian
thought was it from which the Englishmen had drawn their
atheism? It must be admitted that on this point Ascham is a
trifle incoherent. At first he seems to mean that by reading
Italian romances Englishmen had been seduced into a wicked
and profligate course of life, and from this had gone farther, perhaps making the wish father to the thought, to argue that
there was no God. But before long we learn that they make
more account of Tully's *Offices* than of Paul's epistles, and that
they hold the Bible for but a fable. Here certainly he is speaking
of something more than a wicked life brought on by reading
lewd stories and seems to have had in mind rather the type of
doubter who had read the classics not wisely but too well. Finally, the Machiavellian atheist is described clearly and in practically the same terms that continued to be used until the end
of the century.

[2] *The English Works of Roger Ascham,* ed. W. A. Wright, p. 232.

The truth of the matter probably is that the court group of whom Ascham was speaking combined in themselves all the tendencies of free thought then current except the extreme opinions of the religious sects. No mention, to be sure, is made of doubts about immortality, but nevertheless this skeptical current no doubt had an actual if possibly sometimes unrecognized influence. Carefree courtiers were not likely to concern themselves with the abstruse philosophical background of a current of thought or with the scientific data upon which certain conclusions were reached, but would naturally be more interested in practical consequences in life and action. A good part of the free thought and the disrespect for religion then so characteristic of Italy had grown out of the speculations about the soul, but free thought was in the air and English travelers were likely to absorb it without troubling much about its source.

During the ten years following Ascham's attack no important work against atheism appeared, although I think we may conclude that atheism itself, or at least free thought, was making considerable progress.[3] In 1576, however, appeared a rather important work, Bishop John Woolton's tractate, *The Immortalitie of the Soul*. This treatise covers almost the same ground that Rastell's chapter, with which Woolton appears to have been unacquainted, had done forty years before, but it is nevertheless significant for several reasons. For instance, unlike Rastell, Woolton furnishes us with a list of his sources, acknowledging indebtedness to Lactantius, Augustine, Nemesius, Melanchthon, Bullinger, and others. And as we might expect from one who founded himself upon such unimpeachable authorities, his arguments are mostly scriptural, and he freely grants the impossibility of demonstrating immortality by proofs drawn from nature. "Unto this day," he says, "no firme proofe nor evident

[3] In 1572 a certain Carleton sent to Lord Burleigh a *Discourse on the Present State of England*, in which he said: "The realm is divided into three parties, the Papists, the Atheists, and the Protestants. All three are alike favoured; the first and second because, being many, we dare not displease them; the third because, having religion, we fear to displease God in them" (*Calendar of State Papers, Domestic, Addenda, 1566-1579*, p. 439).

demonstration hath ben drawn out of Philosophie to establish and confirme this proposition: *The Soule of man is immortall*."[4]

But he is not opposed to bringing reason to the aid of faith and is willing to furnish natural proofs for those to whom they may make the strongest appeal. The natural proofs that he brings forward, however, we find to be of a most conventional kind. He sees his first duty to be a demonstration of God in his works, and we are asked to observe the orderly motion of the heavens, the certain courses of the stars, and are assured that this regularity bespeaks a divine ruler. He has little to add to what Rastell, or indeed Aristotle and Plato, had said about the soul and its faculties. There are, we are told, really three souls in man, the vegetative, the sensitive, and the rational, only the last of which is immortal. We know that the rational soul is independent of the senses because of its ability to leave the body in thought and in dreams, and from this we can conclude that it does not necessarily perish with the senses and is capable of immortality. Thus he proceeds in a general way to go over the ground that La Primaudaye had already covered so carefully and that Sir John Davies was to cover later. But Woolton is confessedly out of his element in proving immortality by nature and soon returns to the Scripture.

The unbelievers Woolton was refuting were modern ones, whom he mentions and whom he actively engaged in suppressing. The people he mentions whose mouths ought to be stopped are "Jewishe Saduces," no doubt the same group that had caused Hutchinson so much concern, either the Family of Love or the Family of the Mount, "heathenishe Epicures," probably Lucretians or libertines, and "hereticall Anabaptistes." We are also given notice of some philosophers who have said, "To fayth the Soule is Immortall, but to humayne reason it is mortall." This is exactly the position taken by Pomponazzi, and so it seems likely that even if Woolton did not know Pomponazzi by name, he at least knew the thought of his group. He pointed to still another group of unbelievers, however, the followers of

4 Fols. 2–3.

Pliny. After saying that Seneca and Pliny among the ancients had disbelieved in immortality, he adds:

> Would to God he had now a days no folowers, and that as men do both see that Plynie hath erred as well in matters of manners as of nature, and give place unto better opinions, they would also in this matter as little esteme him, seeing that he striveth agaynst all that is called god, against providence, agaynst the blissefull and happie estate of all mankinde, whiles he thus maynteyneth the mortalitie of the soul.[5]

From these considerations it appears that Woolton was the best-informed writer about the state of religious unbelief in England that we have yet studied. He makes no mention of the Machiavellian atheist, it is true, but he was writing on immortality, and the denial of immortality was not a distinctive characteristic of the Machiavellians.

The writers we have been reviewing have been mainly teachers and preachers, but we now come to a member of the very court group about which Ascham was so disturbed, but to one who seems himself to have been considerably influenced by Ascham. This was John Lyly, who in *Euphues: The Anatomy of Wit* (1578) has a section called "Euphues and Atheos," a dialogue between Euphues, the orthodox and scandalized Christian, and Atheos, a rather easily persuaded atheist. Quite unlike Ascham, however, who had been both modern and original, Lyly drew most of his arguments, sometimes almost verbally, from Cicero's *De natura deorum*.

Atheos begins by relating how Diagoras had robbed and insulted the gods in Athens and then returned with a prosperous wind to his own country scoffing at them and adds that if there is a God in his opinion it is nothing but the world. Euphues, after some expressions of horror appropriate to the occasion, rallies himself for a reply. His first proof is the familiar one of universal consent to the existence of God: "The heathen man saith, yea, that Tully whom thou thyself allegest, that there is no nation so barbarous, no kind of people so savage, in whom resteth not this persuasion that there is a God." He next passes

[5] Fol. 54.

to the four reasons that Cicero had put into the mouth of Clean-
tes in *De natura deorum:* first, premonitions of the future that
sometimes come to men; second, the commodities with which
the world is provided necessary for the welfare of men; third,
the terror inspired in us by lightning, earthquakes, and other
natural wonders; and, fourth, the natural order that is seen to
prevail in the universe. Finally, he announces that he will no
longer trifle with philosophy but try the case by Scripture and
proceeds to quote numerous passages that attest the existence
of God.

Atheos promptly objects to the use of the Scripture in the
argument: "Whosoever, therefore, denieth a Godhead denieth
also the Scriptures which testify of Him. This is in my opinion
absurdum per absurdius, to prove one absurdity by another."
Then it devolves upon Euphues to prove the truth of the Scripture, and this he does in such an effective way that Atheos, no
longer able to resist, cries out that he is in mortal terror of being
damned and desires to know the way to salvation. Euphues
obliges him in that particular and closes by saying that Atheos
must now be called Theophilus.

From even this brief summary it is apparent that Lyly had
only a superficial knowledge of the subject with which he was
dealing. He seems to have been fairly certain that there were
atheists in England, and especially at Oxford, where he had proceeded M.A. only three years before. "Be there not many in
Athens,"[6] he asks, "which think there is no God, no redemption,
no resurrection?" And concerning Naples (London) he says,
"There are all things necessary and in readiness that might
either allure the mind to lust or entice the heart to folly: a court
more meet for an atheist than for one of Athens." Again in the
"Epistle to the Gentlemen Scholars of Oxford," prefaced to
"Euphues and Atheos," we are given a possible hint for what he
regarded as atheism when he speaks of "these desperate days
wherein so many sects are sown." But on the whole we must

---

[6] Throughout *Euphues,* Lyly uses Athens to mean Oxford and Naples to mean
London.

conclude that Lyly was rather poorly informed about the unbelief against which he was reacting.

A writer who had a firmer grasp on the points at issue and who was willing to contest the matter on purely philosophical grounds and without the aid of Scripture was Sir Philip Sidney, who in Book III, chapter x, of his *Arcadia* (1582–83), delivered the first reasoned English attack of which we have any record against the mechanistic philosophy of Lucretius. This refutation, imbedded as it is in the rather tedious account of the persecutions of Pamela and Philoclea by the wicked Cecropia, had escaped notice until Edwin Greenlaw called attention to it in his well-informed article, "The Captivity Episode in Sidney's *Arcadia*."[7] I find myself in rather close agreement with Mr. Greenlaw's interpretation of the passage[8] and cannot hope to add much to what he has said, but the completeness of my own study demands here some account of the argument and the conclusions to be drawn from it.

Queen Cecropia, upon the retirement of Basileus from active affairs, was trying to get the realm into her own possession by persuading Pamela to marry Amphialus, Cecropia's son. Annoyed by Pamela's frequent references to God and her conscience, Cecropia studied some means by which she could subvert her from religion, and said:

Dear neece . . . . how much dooth it increase (trowe you) the earnest desire I haue of this blessed match, to see these vertues of yours knit fast with such zeale of Deuotion, indeede the best bonde, which the most politicke wittes haue found, to holde mans witte in well doing? For, as children must first by feare be induced to know that, which after (when they doo know) they are most glad of: So are these bugbeares of opinions brought by great Clearkes into the world. . . . . Feare, and indeede, foolish feare, and fearfull ignorance, was the first inuenter of those conceates. For, when they heard it thunder, not knowing the naturall cause, they thought there was some angrie body aboue, that spake so lowde: and euer the lesse they did perceiue, the more they did conceiue. Whereof they knew no cause that grewe streight a miracle: foolish folks, not marking that the alterations be but vpon particular

---

[7] *Manly Anniversary Studies* (Chicago, 1925), pp. 54–63.

[8] Although I am not so sure that Sidney drew his ideas from Lucretius himself, as Mr. Greenlaw says. Mr. Brie (*op. cit.*, p. 106) thinks that the real source of the passage was Cicero's *De natura deorum*.

accidents, the vniversalitie being alwaies one. . . . . Be wise, and that wise-dome shal be a God vnto thee; be contented, and that is thy heauen: for else to thinke that those powers (if there be any such) aboue, are moued either by the eloquence of our prayers, or in a chafe by the folly of our actions; carries as much reason as if flies should thinke, that men take great care which of them hums sweetest, and which of them flies nimblest.

Pamela replies in a very lively fashion, in fact troubling her-self to refute a number of things that Cecropia had not thought to allege. The constancy of natural law that Cecropia herself had pointed to is in Pamela's opinion evidence of a constant creator, since we know that every effect has a cause and we are led to God as the true cause of all. But Pamela's main argu-ment is against the chance creation of the world taught in the Epicurean philosophy. She marvels by what chance any brain could have stumbled upon such a theory, and specifically in re-gard to the atomic theory of Epicurus declares: "If nothing but Chaunce had glewed those pieces of this All, the heauie partes would haue gone infinitely downewarde, the light infinitely vp-wards, and so neuer haue mett to haue made vp this goodly bodie." The main object of her arguments was, of course, to demonstrate the existence of a providential God, and his exist-ence, Pamela closes her speech by saying, is also to be deduced from the fact that we ourselves are reasonable creatures: "But what madd furie can euer so enueagle any conceipt, as to see our mortall and corruptible selues to haue a reason, and that this vniuersalitie (whereof we are but the lest pieces) should be vtterly deuoide thereof."

The warmth of Sidney's discussion and his familiarity with both sides of the question indicate a more than passing interest in this subject. How may we account for this interest? In my opinion it originated in his absorption at this period with French affairs and was connected with his opposition to the French mar-riage of Queen Elizabeth. If we accept the views of Mr. Green-law, and I am inclined to allow them a good deal of weight, Ce-cropia was meant to represent the queen-mother of France, Catherine de Medici. At this time in disfavor at court for his letter against the marriage with the Duke of Anjou, Sidney may have sought to express himself further under the guise of a romance. Now the court of Catherine was notoriously Machiavellian, and she herself, according to Henri Etienne, was inspired and counseled by Italian atheists before St. Bartholomew's Day. And so it may be that Sidney meant no more than to attribute atheistical beliefs to Catherine and to represent Elizabeth as refuting them. On the other hand, his interest may have been aroused by the prevalence of Epicureanism in France at large. From about 1550 on a revival of Epicureanism in both its practical and its philosophical aspects had continued to be complained of by such writers as Guillaume Postel, Jean de Neufville, and Pierre Viret; and Sidney, who had traveled in France and who always kept well abreast of its affairs, may have known the works of these men and is certain to have known of the existence of the thing they lamented. I do not, of course, mean to preclude the possibility that Sidney could have been aware of Epicureanism in England. It is altogether possible that he was.[9] But since up to this time we have not been informed from any other source of so advanced a mechanistic philosophy among Sidney's own countrymen, and since the utterances given to Cecropia correspond very nearly to the Epicureanism so often described by the French Christian apologists, it seems to me rather likely that in this passage Sidney was reacting to a form of incredulity that existed in France.

The remaining years of the decade were not marked by any long or important attacks on atheism, but there are a few scattered references which may be mentioned in passing and one that should receive at least cursory attention. Philip Stubbs, writing in his *Anatomie of Abuses* in 1583, tells us that there are some who think hell but a fable or metaphorical way of speaking and who make a mock of the idea of future rewards and punishments. One year later Thomas Cooper in his *Admonition to the People of England* discovered a cause for atheism in the clergy themselves, who had been giving strange interpretations to the

9 Worth mentioning in this connection is the fact that his rival, Edward de Vere, the seventeenth Earl of Oxford, was an Italianate gentleman of a rather pronounced type and a few years later was being charged with "horrible and detestable blasphemy," "irreverence to the Scriptures," and "atheism" (*Calendar of State Papers, Domestic, 1581–1590*, Nos. 45, 49, 57).

articles of the common creed, particularly to the article that
concerned Christ's descent into hell. He then says:

These and a number of other such, have undoubtedly bred great offence,
and wounded the hearts of an infinite number, causing them partly to revolt
to Papistry, partly to Atheisme, and neglecting of all Religion, as is seene by
the lives of many, to the exceeding griefe of all them that feare God and love
his truth.[10]

In 1588 John Udall, writing in his *Demonstration of Discipline*,
had similar charges to bring against the "Svpposed Gouernours
of the Church of England, the Archbyshops, lord Byshops,
Archdeacons, and the rest of that order." These, in his opinion,
with their love of pomp had brought about most of the evils of
the church. He adds:

And the greatest of your fault appeareth in this, that in so doing, you are
the cause of all the ignorance, Atheisme, schisme, treason, poperie and vn-
godliness, that is to be found in this land. . . . . That you are the cause of all
atheisme, it is plaine, for one may (as in deede many doe) professe it, and you
saye nothing to him for it.[11]

During the early years of the decade the redoubtable Gabriel
Harvey had begun to express himself in the vigorous fashion he
ever after affected about various matters of common interest,
and it would be surprising if the question of atheism had escaped his attention. His first reference to the subject, although
not very immediate, opens up for our study a field of inquiry
that has thus far not been touched upon, that is, how far the
new conception of the world brought about by the voyages of
Columbus and Magellan and the discoveries of Copernicus and
his followers was undermining faith in the Christian scheme. It
was the tendency, closely related to the new science, to assign
more and more things to natural causes that had annoyed Harvey, and in a letter to Spenser discussing the cause of the earth-
quake of 1580 he seized the occasion to denounce too much pry-
ing into the mysteries of the universe:

I cannot see, and would gladly learne, how a man on Earth, should be of
so great authoritie, and so familiar acquaintance with God in Heauen (vnlesse
haply for the nonce he hath lately intertained some fewe choice singular ones

10 Arber reprint, p. 15.   11 *Ibid.*, p. 4.

of his priuie Counsell) as to be able in such specialties, without any iustifyable certificate, or warrant to reueale hys incomprehensible mysteries, and definitiuely to giue sentence of his Maiesties secret and inscrutable purpose. As if they had a key for all the lockes in Heauen.[12]

One of the most surprising things to a student beginning a study of sixteenth-century England is the fact that general writers and the population at large seem to have been unconscious of or not much interested in the revolutionary and era marking discoveries of such pioneers as Magellan and Copernicus. It is not hard to go through the period and pick out quotations from this or that person showing that he knew pretty well what was going on, and certainly the prompt action of the Holy See against Galileo and Bruno shows beyond doubt that those whose interests were most closely concerned were keeping well abreast of the scientific thought of the day. Yet it is none the less true that the new ideas did not rapidly become current and that they did not become subjects for popular controversy until a much later day. There has been much speculation on this point, usually by men who have not burdened their minds with much reading from original sources, and it does seem as if the new science should have been an important factor in religious unbelief at least by 1575. But I do not find it to have been so from my reading in the general literature of the period, and, consequently, in spite of such isolated reactions as the one we have just noted from Harvey, I do not regard the scientific discoveries as a major source for religious incredulity in England prior to 1600.

[12] *Harvey's Works*, ed. Grosart, I, 56–57.

VII

The Reaction (1590-1600)
Greene, Nashe, Harvey, Lodge, Hooker, Beard, Bacon

W E NOW come to a consideration of that extraordinarily vigorous and articulate group of Cambridge men who sprang suddenly into literary prominence shortly before the year 1590. They made signal contributions to English literature in almost every field, but they also made England clamorous with their quarrels, repentances, quips, charges and countercharges, and their lives and quarrels moved so rapidly and in so complex a pattern that the student is almost baffled in the attempt to follow them. This group consisted of Gabriel Harvey, Robert Greene, Thomas Nashe, and Christopher Marlowe, all of whom touch our subject at some place, for they were all concerned in the question of atheism. Harvey repeatedly accused Nashe and others, tossing the charge about in a reckless way; Greene was a confessed atheist on his deathbed and accused Marlowe; and Nashe himself wrote a stirring attack on atheism, giving its causes and minute directions for its suppression. Of these we shall consider Greene, Nashe, and Harvey at this time, Marlowe being reserved for fuller treatment in a subsequent chapter.

Greene's attack is closely connected with his own atheism, from which he represents himself as repenting, and with Marlowe's. Already in *Perimedes the Blacksmith* (1588) he had referred to some poet's "daring God out of heauen with that Atheist Tamburlan," meaning Marlowe of course, but in *Groats-Worth of Wit* (1592), one of the repentance pieces, he becomes much more explicit. Here Greene, aware of his approaching death, addresses a letter "To those Gentlemen his Quondam acquaintance, that spend their wits in making plaies" and urges them to give over their questionable trade and repent of their sins. He begins with Marlowe:

> Wonder not, (for with thee wil I first begin) thou famous gracer of Tragedians, that Greene, who hath said with thee (like the foole in his heart) There is no God, shoulde now giue glorie vnto his greatnes: for penetrating is his power, his hand lyes heauie vpon me. . . . . Why should thy excellent wit, his gift, bee so blinded, that thou shouldst giue no glorie to the giuer? Is it pestilent Machiuilian pollicy that thou hast studied? O peeuish follie! What are his rules but meere confused moskeries, able to extirpate in small time the generations of mankind? . . . . The brocher of this Diabolicall Atheisme is dead, and in his life had neuer the felicitie hee aymed at: but as he began in craft; liued in feare, and ended in dispaire. *Quam inscrutabilia sunt Dei iudicia?* This murderer of many brethern, had his conscience seared like Caine: This betrayer of him that gaue his life for him, inherited the portion of Iudas: this Apostata perished as ill as Iulian; and wilt thou my friend be his disciple? Looke but to me, by him perswaded to that libertie, and thou shalt find it an infernall bondage.[1]

Thus we are furnished not only with the information that Marlowe was an atheist but also with the source of his unbelief, the works of Machiavelli. Indeed, Greene admits that he also had been misled by reading Machiavelli, "by him perswaded to that libertie," and so there ought not, I think, to be any doubt about the identity of at least two of the "odd crewe or tooe" mentioned by Harvey who at Cambridge were so proficient in the works of Machiavelli.

But Machiavelli was not the only source for either Marlowe's or Greene's attitude toward religion. Near the end of the letter in *Groats-Worth of Wit*, speaking to all the playwrights he had addressed, Greene urges them to "Abhorre those Epicures, whose loose life hath made religion lothsome to your eares." Whether this Epicureanism was one of philosophy or of mere practice Greene does not say, but it is to be suspected that it was largely the latter. Greene's description of his own course of life renders this view plausible, for if we may believe his accounts in *The Repentance of Robert Greene* (1592), his youth had been one of

---

[1] Grosart, *Greene's Works*, XII, 142. It will be noticed that Greene had a most distorted idea of Machiavelli's life.

almost unparalleled depravity. "Well, at that time," he says, "whosoeuer was worst, I knew my selfe as bad as he: for being new come from Italy, (where I learned all the villanies vnder heauens) I was drowned in pride, whoredome was my daily exercise, and gluttony with drunkennes was my onely delight."

Nevertheless it is clear enough that Greene meant to represent himself as an actual atheist and not merely as a wicked and profligate man. He had said with Marlowe, "There is no God," and he says in another connection, "For my contempt of God, I am contemned of men." His temper, and perhaps the temper of his group as well, is probably best shown by a passage in the *Repentance*. There he says that once when some friend had given him moral advice he replied, "If I may haue my desire while I liue, I am satisfied, let me shift after death as I may." His friend then reminded him of hell, and he merely replied that if it should be his fate to go there he should meet better men than himself.

Now as to whether Greene exaggerated his religious attitude and the wickedness of his youth for dramatic reasons, in order to make a good story, it is impossible to determine, since almost all of our information about his life is gathered from these autobiographical works. But it is a noteworthy fact that his contemporaries accepted the revelations as genuine, and his charges against Marlowe are corroborated from other sources. The important thing, however, is that Greene's repentance works taken together constitute a vigorous reaction to contemporary atheism, an atheism apparently of Machiavellian origin, but complicated by other factors such as Epicureanism, mere wickedness and debauchery, and a contemptuous, scoffing attitude toward all religion. We are moreover led to infer the existence of two groups holding atheistical opinions: first, the literary men of London, most of them from the universities, where they had become acquainted with Machiavelli and with irreligious thought from other sources; second, a group of London Epicures, no doubt comprising political hangers-on, petty criminals, and the general unprincipled riffraff of a large city.

And from the lives of Greene and Marlowe we also find reason
to believe that the line between these groups was not very clearly drawn.

The most complete and detailed analysis, if not always the
most trustworthy, of the whole question of atheism furnished us
by any English writer before 1600 came from the pen of Greene's
friend Thomas Nashe, who like Greene was himself accused of
atheism in very positive terms by their common enemy, Gabriel Harvey. Nashe's attack is contained in two pamphlets,
Pierce Penilesse (1592) and *Christs Teares over Jerusalem* (1593),
and it is in the second of these that the first point we should
notice is taken up. Like many others, Nashe had been struck
by the fact that atheists were exceedingly numerous. While
calling on the preachers to combat atheism, he says: "There is
no Sect now in England so scattered as Atheisme. . . . . You
are not halfe so wel acquainted as them that lyue continually
about the Court and City, how many followers this damnable
paradoxe hath: how many high wits it hath bewitcht."[2]

But equally interesting for us are the causes for atheism that
Nashe saw fit to mention from time to time. On this point he
is extremely voluble—in fact, so voluble that we are unable to
make very much of what he says. His fault may have been ignorance, exaggeration, or indifference, but whatever it was, it
led him to give contradictory statements and one or two that
are patently absurd. From *Pierce Penilesse* we learn of three
causes—rationalism, the works of Aristotle, and the warfare of
the sects:

Some men there be that building too much vpon reason, perswade themselues that there are no Diuels at all; but that this word *Daemon*, is such
another morall of mischiefe, as the poets Dame Fortune.

Whence, a number that fetch the Articles of their Beleefe out of Aristotle,
and thinke of heauen and hell as the Heathen Philosophers, take occasion to
deride our Ecclesiasticall State, and all Ceremonies of Deuine worship, as
bugbeares scarcrows, because (like Herodes souldiers) we diuide Christs
garments amongst vs.

[2] R. B. McKerrow, *The Works of Thomas Nashe*, II, 121-22.

From *Christs Teares*, of three more—prosperity, superabund-ance of wit, and dull preachers:

> 'Tis nothing but plenty and abundance that makes men Atheists.
> These Atheists (with whom you are to encounter) are speciall men of witte.
> . . . . It is the superaboundance of witte that makes Atheists.
> It is onely ridiculous dul Preachers . . . . that have reuiued thys scornefull Sects of Atheists.

And from the *Unfortunate Traveller*, of one—Italian travel:

> Italy, the Paradice of the earth and the Epicures heaven, how doth it form our yong master? . . . . From thence he brings the art of atheisme, the art of epicurizing.

Nashe perhaps did not give as much thought to this matter as we could wish he had, but it would be a mistake to underesti-mate what he has to say. He is too well corroborated by other writers for us not to believe that when he connected atheism with Aristotle, Italy, and the struggle of the sects he had hit upon the truth.

Nashe's method for suppressing and rooting out atheism is not a very original one, but it is hard to see what other he could have suggested. He appeals to the clergy to drop minor con-troversies and bend all efforts against this greater danger: "Uni-versity men that are called to preache at the Crosse and the Court, Arme yourselves against nothing but Atheisme, meddle not so much with Sects and forraine opinions, but let Atheisme be the onely string you beate on." In his directions for carrying on this warfare he shows a good deal of acumen. It was his opinion that too much time at the universities was being given to the study of Bible commentaries. The clergy ought rather to study the same profane authors from which the atheists had de-rived their beliefs, since it was mere folly to quote the Bible to atheists. "Skyrmishing with atheists," he says, "you must be-have your selves as you were converting Gentiles."

Whatever their differences on other matters, Nashe and Har-vey were certainly at one in deploring the presence of atheism in England. The difference here was that Harvey thought Nashe himself and his group were all atheists. In fact, his remarks about religious unbelief are practically all confined to charges against Nashe, Greene, Marlowe, and their associates. In his *New Letter of Notable Content* (1593) he says:

> Plinyes and Lucians religion may ruffle, and scoffe awhile: but extreme Vanitie is the best beginning of that brauery, and extreme Miserie the best end of that felicity. Greene and Marlow might admonish other to aduise themselues.[3]

And about this time he begins to call Nashe Aretine:

> Though Greene were a Iulian and Marlowe a Lucian: yet I would be loth, He should be an Aretine: that Paraphrased the inestimable bookes of Moses and discoursed the Capricious Dialogues of rankest Bawdry . . . . that recorded the history of S. Thomas of Aquine, and forged the most detestable Blackebooke *de tribus impostoribus mundi*.[4]

In *An Advertisement for Papp-hatchett* (1593) he is again comparing Nashe to Aretine as well as giving other interesting information:

> They neither feare Goodman Sathan, nor master Beelzebub, nor Sir Reuerence, nor milord Gouernement himselfe: O wretched Atheisme, Hell but a scarecrow, and Heauen but a woonder-clout in their doctrine: all vulgar, stale, and simple, that is not a note abooue Goddes-forbid. . . . . Whom will he [Nashe] forbeare, in any reason, of conscience, that hath often protested in his familiar hauntes, to confute the worthy Lord du Bartas.

It is refreshing to know that there was one person in England not completely enamored with Du Bartas's "sugar'd lines" but a pity that Harvey could not tell us how Nashe meant to set about his confutation.

Now any attempt to evaluate the trustworthiness of Harvey's statement is of course made difficult by the fact that he was engaged in a bitter quarrel with Nashe and his group and would thus have been tempted to exaggerate any bit of information that would represent his enemies in an unfavorable light. He was careless of facts, as we have seen in his positive ascription

---

[3] Grosart, *Harvey's Works*, I, 289–90.

[4] For a discussion of this work see the chapter on Marlowe's atheism. It was variously ascribed to Averroes, Frederick II, Boccaccio, Aretino, Machiavelli, Erasmus, Servetus, Pomponazzi, Rabelais, Bruno, Vanini, Hobbes, Spinoza, and others, but whether any such work every really existed before the eighteenth century is still in doubt. The impostors referred to were Moses, Christ, and Mohammed.

of *De tribus impostoribus* to Aretino, but that he would have invented evidence, even to harm Nashe, I do not believe. Indeed, he anticipated the charge of exaggeration and wished it to be known that he was not telling even all he knew. Speaking of Greene, he says, "If I knew no more than I vtter; I would hope no lesse, then I wish." It must also be kept in mind that he said no more about Marlowe than Greene and Kyd had said and not as much as Baines, and that he accused Greene of nothing that Greene himself did not admit. Then it is at least probable that his charges against Nashe had some foundation in fact.

If Harvey was guilty of exaggeration it was more than likely in the interpretation he placed on what he had seen and heard. I do not believe the so-called atheism of either Greene or Nashe ran very deep or was a settled conviction reached after a long period of deliberation. It was a mood or temper, out of which they were easily shaken. They were, according to Harvey, followers of Pliny, Julian, Lucian, Machiavelli, and Epicurus. At various times they probably toyed with opinions derived from all of these, but they were not very serious. Lewis and Kett went to the stake for their atheism, the denial of Christ's divinity, and, on the Continent, Dolet and Bruno, although for different forms of unbelief, shared the same fate. Greene and Nashe and their companions were not men of this mettle. In atheism they were dilettantes.

In the same eventful year (1593) appeared another work of a most promising title for our subject, *God's Arrow against Atheism*, by the preacher Henry Smith, but it turns out on examination to be a very negligible performance. Although divided into six chapters, it is really no more than an elongated sermon and conforms to that type in nearly every particular. Smith proves the existence of God, confutes the Gentiles and infidels of the world, displays the religion of Mohammed as false and wicked, and attacks the Catholics and sectaries. But the arguments are almost all scriptural or theological and the only atheists named are those of antiquity. Smith had evidently heard that there was much atheism in England, but he knew almost nothing about it and spoke in the vaguest terms until he came to the chapter against the Catholics. He conforms exactly to the type of preacher described by Nashe in *Christs Teares*, and it seems to me not improbable that Nashe had him personally in mind.

Much closer in touch with actual conditions was Thomas Lodge, who in *Wits Miserie, and the Worlds Madnesse* (1595), incident to his description of the common vices, tells us a good deal about atheism and the men who profess it. He describes the devil Derision, for instance, in the following terms:

He neuer sitteth but in the chaire of Pestilence, his meerest profession is Atheisme: and as Iob saith, to mock at the simplicitie of the iust. . . . . Christ his Sauior is a Carpenters sonne: Christians, Galileans in contempt: Nay such blasphemie he vttereth betwixt the Holy ghost and the blessed and Immaculate Virgine Marie, as my heart trembleth to thinke them, and my tongue abhorreth to speake them.[5]

According to the Baines report, Marlowe had made statements almost identical with these, that Christ was the son of a carpenter and that if the Jews among whom he was born did crucify him, they knew him best and whence he came, that the angel Gabriel was bawd to the Holy Ghost because he brought the salutation to Mary. So it seems that from some source Lodge became aware of Marlowe's opinions, possibly from the Baines report, possibly from Marlowe himself.

In 1597 we come to a well-informed attack on atheism in that powerful defense of the Anglican establishment, *The Laws of Ecclesiastical Polity* by Richard Hooker. It is in Book V, section 2, of this that Hooker turns to a brief consideration of the atheism so often denounced, and here we learn that for all his elevation of reason to the highest attribute of God or man, he is not a whit more tolerant toward a state of mind in which reason plays so large a part. He escaped this inconsistency to his own satisfaction, however, in professing to see no reason in atheism, unless the mere rationalization of low desires could be called reason. Yet his treatment of the subject as a whole, in spite of the Ciceronian cadence of his style, is somewhat more sober and

[5] Edmund Gosse, *The Works of Thomas Lodge*, IV, 10–11.

restrained than we have been accustomed to hear, and his air of being on familiar ground, combined with a good deal of penetration, persuades us into the belief that we should allow much truth to what he has to say.

At the beginning of the section he divides atheists into two groups: the first, wholly negligible in number, men who have no apprehension of a God; the second and important group, those who for reasons of their own wish to believe there is no God. The radical or ultimate cause of the atheism of this second group, Hooker declares, is the desire to reap all the pleasures of this world without any thought of the future. He then says:

And that this is the very radical cause of their Atheism no man (I think) will doubt, which considereth what pains they take to destroy their principal spurs and motives unto all virtue, the Creation of the World, the Providence of God, the Resurrection of the Dead, the Joys of the Kingdom of Heaven, and the endless Pains of the Wicked, yea, above all things, the Authority of the Scripture, because on these points it evermore beateth, and the Soul's Immortality, which granted, draweth easily after it the rest as a voluntary train.

The list of these "principal spurs and motives unto all virtue" that the atheists were attempting to destroy almost summarizes the whole question of religious unbelief for the latter part of the century. The biblical account of the creation was questioned by those who followed Aristotle in believing the world eternal and by those who thought with Epicurus and Lucretius that it had been created by chance. The providence of God was denied by the disciples of Pliny and Lucretius. The resurrection was denied and heaven and hell declared allegorical by the English Sadducees, that is, by the Family of Love and the sects of a like order. The doubts of immortality had stemmed down from Aristotle through such commentators as Averroes and had been revived principally by the University of Padua. That any special group was denying the validity of the Scripture or developing a form of higher criticism we have not yet observed, but such a denial was a necessary concomitant of belief in Lucretius or Pliny, or even a belief in Aristotle as interpreted by Alexander of Aphrodisias or Pomponazzi. Nor is there any reason to suppose that disbelief in the Scripture was limited to followers of these men. A good deal of faith is needed to believe all that is set down in the Bible, and it would be no great intellectual feat for an Englishman with his own unaided reason to arrive at the conclusion that it was not divinely inspired.

The followers of Machiavelli had escaped any reference in Hooker's first list, but that he was not in the least ignorant of them and their beliefs the following passage is a sufficient witness:

> They would fain believe that the hearty devotion of such as indeed fear God, is nothing else but a kind of harmless error, bred and confirmed in them by the slights of wiser men. For a politic use of Religion they see there is, and by it they would also gather that Religion itself is a mere politic device, forged purposely to serve for that use. . . . . They give it out as a mystical precept of great importance, that the Princes and such as are under them in most authority and credit with the people, should take all occasion of rare events, and from what cause soever the same do proceed, yet wrest them to the strengthening of their Religion, and not make it nice for so good a purpose to use, if need be, plain forgeries. Thus while they study to bring to pass that Religion may seem but a matter made, they lose themselves in the very maze of their own discourses, as if Reason did even purposely forsake them, who of purpose forsake God, the author thereof.

The opinions here attributed to atheists are exactly those expressed in chapters xi–xiv of the *Discourses upon Titus Livius*, where Numa Pompilius is praised for inventing the Roman religion and for having the shrewdness to give out that it was revealed to him by a nymph, and where the Roman leaders are represented as consistently inventing miracles and taking advantage of religion in various ways to effect their own ends.

Hooker is a writer who inspires a good deal of confidence. There are times, to be sure, when we are not able to follow him all the way, as when he says that the radical cause of atheism is the desire to share all the pleasures of the world, but when wrong he is usually very obviously wrong and the reader is thus not likely to be misled. What he tells us about the sources of atheism and the nature of atheists we are constrained to believe, and it is with reluctance that we turn to a man who, although zealous enough, was not endowed with his clarity of vision.

This was Thomas Beard, the Puritan divine who was later to train the young Oliver Cromwell in his grammar school, and who in 1597 favored the world with a remarkable book which he called *The Theatre of Gods Judgements*. As the title implies, the work was designed to show that, contrary to popular belief, God did not make a practice of delaying punishment of notable offenders until the future life and that wicked men could look forward to a good deal of punishment in this world. To accomplish this worthy purpose Beard ran over ancient and modern history, secular and ecclesiastical, selected great personages who had been guilty of murder, adultery, incest, atheism, apostacy, and other crimes, and showed, with the kind of logic that anyone who reads morals into human suffering is obliged to adopt, that their subsequent misfortunes were the results of these crimes. Beard's book has long been known for its description of the death of Marlowe,[6] but it is the entire chapter in which this occurs, chapter xxiii, "Of Epicures, and Atheists," that relates to our subject.

Beard begins his chapter by averring that "Epicures and cursed Atheists, that denie the prouidence of God, beleeue not the immortalitie of the soule, thinke there is no such thing as life to come, and consequently impugne all diuinity, liuing in this world like brute beasts." Like many another he is able to trace the origin of English atheism to Italy, but he goes farther than most and finds the Catholic church to be largely responsible for it. The chief promoters of atheism in Italy, says Beard, had been men of no less ecclesiastical importance than Pope Leo X, Pope Julian III, and Cardinal Bembo.

Coming nearer home, he lists four important French atheists —Francis Rabelais, who had made all religion a matter of scorn and who had died mad; Des Periers, who had written the de-

---

[6] A description that the researches of Mr. Leslie Hotson (*The Death of Christopher Marlowe* [Harvard University Press, 1925]) have shown to correspond pretty closely to the truth, or at least to the coroner's report.

testable book *Symbolum mundi*, wherein he openly mocked at God and religion; Jodelle, the tragical French poet; and the courtier Ligneroles, who made open profession of atheism. Among the English only one is mentioned by name.:

Not inferior to any of the former in Atheisme and impiety, and equal to al in maner of punishment, was one of our own nation, of fresh and late memorie, called Marlin, by profession a scholler, brought vp from his youth in the Vniuersitie of Cambridge, but by practice a Play-maker, and a poet of scurrilitie, who by giving too large a swing to his owne wit, and suffering his lust to haue the full reines, fell (not without just desert) to that outrage and extremetie, that hee denied God, and his sonne Christ, and not onely blasphemed the Trinitie, but also (as it is credibly reported) wrote bookes against it, affirming our Sauior to be but a deceiuer, and Moses to be but a coniurer and seducer of the people, and the holy Bible to bee but a vaine and idle storie, and all religion but a deuice of policie.

Following the Marlowe passage, Beard refers to another English atheist, a gentleman in Berkshire whom he prefers not to name, so far gone in iniquity as once at a christening actually to suggest that the child be called Beelzebub. In view of this and his other enormities Beard was not surprised when he heard that this man had been struck dead while riding to a hunt and was taken down from his horse with his tongue hanging out of his mouth in a fearful manner.

The question of atheism was not one likely to escape the attention of the greatest philosopher of his day and the father of modern science, Francis Bacon. Yet his interest in it seems to have been rather slight, and it must be admitted that his comments as a whole are not especially enlightening. It is true that he made one famous statement on the subject, the one about a little science inclining a man toward atheism but much study bringing him back again to religion—famous not so much for its truth, which is seriously open to question, but because it was to become a rallying cry for the Christian apologists at a later time when the defenders of the faith were to find themselves closely pressed by the forces of science. This statement, however, whether half true or wholly false, was almost his only contribution to the subject.

Bacon treated the question briefly in his *Meditationes sacrae*

(1597)[7] when along with such topics as "Hypocrites" and "Heresies" he introduced a short essay, "Of Atheism," taking as his text, "The fool hath said in his heart, There is no God." Here we are first told of the enthusiasm and frenzy that possess those seduced to atheism:

There is no heresy which strives with more zeal to spread and sow and multiply itself, than Atheism. Nor shall you see those who are fallen into this phrenzy to breathe and importunately inculcate anything else almost, than speech tending to Atheism: as in Lucretius the Epicurean; who makes his invective against religion almost as the burthen or verse of return to every other subject.[8]

Bacon then proceeds to divide atheists into three kinds—first, the light, scoffing type we have so often met before; second, the political atheist, the atheistical statesman who ascribes everything to his own powers and nothing to God; third, the scientist:

Thirdly, in physics likewise, I maintain this—that a little natural philosophy and the first entrance into it inclines men's opinions to Atheism; but on the other hand much natural philosophy and a deeper progress into it brings men's minds about again to religion.

Concerning the existence of scientific atheists, we have been furnished with a hint or two before, but so far as I know this was the first time it was definitely stated in England that a study of science was conducive to atheism. The statement naturally comes with added force from Bacon, for it is to be supposed that he knew as much about the subject as any man of his age.

[7] Translated into English in 1598.

[8] *The Works of Francis Bacon* (London, 1859), VII, 251.

VIII

The Translations (1561-1605)
Calvin, Bullinger, Viret, La Primaudaye,
La Noue, Mornay, Du Bartas

THERE can be no doubt but that the translation into English of a large number of Continental attacks on religious incredulity is very intimately connected with the English reaction to atheism and other forms of religious unbelief. It would be a mistake to conclude hastily that the translation of these works first called attention of the English to the existence of free thought, for we have seen that atheism, and especially the atheism that took the form of the denial of immortality, was being vigorously attacked by such writers as Rastell and Latimer long before these translations began to be made. And indeed it would seem that unless there had been some local interest in the phenomenon, the translation of the works devoted exclusively to the problem would perhaps never have been made at all.[1] But we are not likely to overestimate their importance. They served to emphasize a matter that had been receiving only sporadic or cursory attention from English writers, they crystallized English thought on the subject, they became arsenals from which English writers drew their weapons, and they inspired works of a similar nature from English pens. It is surely not without significance that the concerted English attack did not begin until after Gentillet, La Primaudaye, and Mornay had been translated, and it may be wondered if the atheism of Marlowe and Raleigh and their associates would not have passed

[1] Nor should it be forgotten that the general reading of a candidate for holy orders and probably of most university students as well would include the early Church Fathers Augustine, Lactantius, and Nemesius, all of whom, in the neo-Platonic tradition, felt the necessity of defending the immortality of the soul.

without so much comment if the minds of their contemporaries had not first been stirred up by the works of the French Christian apologists.

In the compass of one chapter it would of course not be possible to discuss every translated work that is in any way related to our subject, even if they were all known and available. The most important and influential ones, however, fortunately still known and accessible, are the works of Calvin, Bullinger, Gentillet, Viret, La Primaudaye, La Noue, Mornay, and Du Bartas, and to these we shall necessarily confine our attention.

The first of these in point of time was John Calvin, who in the first book of the *Institutes of the Christian Religion*, translated by Thomas Norton in 1561, gave several chapters to demonstrating the existence of God, to discussing the nature and faculties of the soul, and to proving immortality.[2] In the third chapter of this book, under the title "The Knowledge of God Naturally Implanted in the Human Mind," Calvin proceeds to run over some of the main arguments of Cicero's *De natura deorum*. The belief in a deity is a natural instinct placed in man by God himself, and there is no nation so barbarous, no race so brutish, as not to share the conviction that there is a God. Calvin then says:

> It is most absurd, therefore, to maintain, as some do, that religion was devised by the cunning and craft of a few individuals, as a means of keeping the body of the people in due subjection, while there was nothing which those very individuals, while teaching others to worship God, less believed than the existence of a God.

He finally points out that atheism is a state of mind reached in spite of man's natural instincts, and that such men as Diagoras and Dionysius have lived in constant fear and have been the prey of troubled consciences.

Calvin was ready enough to admit the existence of atheism in his day, saying, "In old times there were some, and in the present day not a few are found who deny the being of a God." Concerning these moderns he is more definite when he comes to a

---

[2] I have used the translation of Henry Beveridge (Edinburgh, 1895).

discussion of the soul. Here, in chapter v, although mentioning no names, he undoubtedly refers to the Paduans. He had been refuting the Epicureans and turned from them to say:

> But my business at present is not with that stye: I wish rather to deal with those who, led away by absurd subtleties, are inclined, by giving an indirect turn to the frigid doctrine of Aristotle, to employ it for the purpose both of disproving the immortality of the soul and robbing God of his rights. Under the pretext that the faculties of the soul are organized, they chain it to the body as if it were incapable of a separate existence, while they endeavour as much as in them lies, by pronouncing eulogiums on nature, to suppress the name of God.

To refute these absurdities Calvin deems it sufficient to say that measuring the heavens, calculating the speed of the stars, and describing their orbits are tasks too lofty to be performed by a body alone, and that the swift movements of the soul in glancing from heaven to earth, its skill in inventing so many arts, its activity when the body is asleep, and its presentiment of things to come are clear indications of immortality.

There is little direct evidence that Calvin's summary of the proofs for the existence of God and for the immortality of the soul had any particular influence in England. He had been reacting to French and Italian unbelief, especially to the Paduans, and he may have called the attention of English readers to the fact that the immortality of the soul was by no means a closed question. Widely read as he was in England, he no doubt aroused some interest in the question of atheism and prepared the way for the more detailed works that were to follow.

The year 1577 saw two important translations. The first of these, Simon Patericke's translation of Innocent Gentillet's *Contre-Machiavel*, has already been discussed in the chapter on Machiavelli and may be omitted from consideration here. The other was Henry Bullinger's *Decades*, first published at Zurich in 1550, a work consisting of ten volumes of sermons on almost every point of the reformed Christian doctrine. Since the days of Mary, when he had sheltered and aided the English exiles at Zurich, Bullinger had continued to enjoy high favor with English divines, and this translation of the *Decades*, as Strype tells us,[3] was meant to serve the purpose of such clergymen as lacked the time or ability to compose sermons of their own. Thus it was in effect an authorized book of homilies and must in time have been read by almost every clergyman in England.

It is in the tenth sermon of the Fourth Decade that Bullinger takes up a discussion of the soul and its faculties and defends the idea of immortality. He reflects on the Aristotelians, who deny that the soul is a substance, saying that it is nothing but the power of life in a man and thus a certain quality, and himself offers the definition that it "is a spiritual substance, poured of God into man's body, that, being joined thereunto, it might quicken and direct the same; but being divorced from the body, it should not die but live immortal forever."[4] He also, like Calvin, refutes the old idea of the unity of souls taught by Aristotle and some of his followers: "We do not allow of them who, minding to express what manner of substance the soul is, say that the soul is God, or else surely a part or portion of God. For the scripture reproveth them both."

Having already studied the contributions of several preachers, we are not surprised when we find that Bullinger draws most of his proofs for immortality from the Bible. He was none too confident of his method, however, and was vaguely aware that it was open to attack. Once he retorted sharply: "They are fleshly therefore and brutish altogether which are not ashamed to say, That they cannot be persuaded or brought to believe the immortality of souls by the scriptures alone." But finally, evidently for the sake of these brutish people, he condescends to point out that all the wise men of the Gentiles—Pythagoras, Plato, Seneca, Epictetus, and others—have believed the soul immortal, that the belief is imprinted by nature on the minds of men and has the universal consent of all nations. In the face of all this evidence, "If there be as yet any light-headed men, to whom the immortality of the soul seemeth doubtful, or which utterly deny the same, these truly are unworthy to have the name of men; for they are plagues of the commonwealth, and

[3] *Annals*, II, ii, 444-45.   [4] Parker Society ed., IV, 368.

very beasts, worthy to be hissed and driven out of the company of men."

A work of minor interest and of an altogether different nature from the ones we have just noticed is Pierre Viret's *Worlde Possessed with Deuils*, translated into English by T. S. in 1583. This is a series of dialogues, quite in the tone of Philip Stubb's *Anatomy of Abuses* (1583) and Thomas Lodge's *Wits Miserie and the Worlds Madnesse* (1595), treating of the various kinds of devils, white, black, familiar, and lunatic, that have overrun the world and possessed so many worldly and carnal men. Along with the detailed accounts of the wickedness brought into the world by these monsters who take the form of men Viret inserts several passages in which libertines, Epicures, and atheists are railed upon in exactly the fashion that soon became popular in England. This sect of atheists seems in Viret's opinion to have derived their heresy mostly from too much reading of pagan authors, and according to him one learned group was denying the truth of the Scripture:

There are such a number of Poeticall braynes, & so learned in the tongues and in humayne Philosophy: that they doe not onely make smal accompt of the books of the holy Scriptures, in comparison of their Heathinishe volumes: as that, which is of all other the most vyle, they esteeme of them no better, then of the Dreames of olde doatyng fooles, and of doating olde wyues tales. And as for mine own part, let them haue as great knowledge as they will, vntill they burst withall, I wil esteem of them no whit the more, if they be not honest men, and haue the feare of God before their eyes.[5]

There was another group, however, which manifested its atheism by temporizing and following out the precepts of Machiavelli. These people, he says, are willing to become "a Papist amongst Papists, an Epicure with Epicures, an Atheist with Atheistes, and to be shorte, a Diuel amongst Diuels, for they wil not be disquited eyther in body or mynd neyther yet hazarde eyther bodye or goodes." Viret then continues to rail against atheists for several paragraphs, without descending to particulars, and finally closes by comparing the learned men of his time

---

[5] Fol. D5. I am indebted to Mr. Merritt Williams of the California Institute of Technology for a careful summary of the Huntington Library copy of Viret's work.

to Augustine before his conversion, and by saying they should be considered as pagans and not as Christians, since they have sucked their opinions from the books of Epicurus.

In 1586 was translated into English that interminable book of Pierre de la Primaudaye, the *French Academie*, first published at Paris in 1557 and re-edited in 1580. This enormous work, almost of encyclopedic proportions, contained an "Institute of Good Manners," a "Natural Historie of the Body and Soule," and a "Notable Description of the Whole World," but fortunately it is only with the second that we need concern ourselves. A great deal of this section is given over to information of a purely anatomical nature, like Nemesius' *De natura hominis* and Lactantius' *De opificio dei*, although much fuller; but with these matters disposed of, La Primaudaye turns to a consideration of the soul and furnishes us with an extraordinarily detailed analysis of its nature and functions. Amid this wealth of learning about the body and soul, which I shall not attempt to summarize, the reader is likely to forget what La Primaudaye's object in writing the book really was. Yet he had stated it clearly enough at the beginning of the second part:

We are now to call to memorie all the testimonies that wee can bring of God and his prouidence, of his iudgement, and of the immortalitie of mens soules, by the consideration of the nature of man, and of his parts. . . . . For no doubt but such kind of contemplation will furnish vs sufficiently with arguments to conuince all Epicures and Atheists, and to constraine them to acknowledge in their conscience a diuine iustice, and an eternall life.[6]

These Epicures and atheists were clearly in need of confutation if we may believe La Primaudaye in regard to their numbers, for unless he exaggerated they outnumbered the good Christians. Near the beginning of the *Second Part* he says, "There are many, yea moe at this day that doe openly shewe themselues to be Atheists and Epicures, then there are of those that are taken for good Christians."

The opinions of the atheists of La Primaudaye's time seem to have been drawn principally from the classics: "As for the writings of Philosophers, they will beleeue *Epicurus, Pliny, Lu-*

[6] I use the edition of 1618.

cretius, *Lucian*, and others of their sect, who deny all deuinity, and the immortality of soules." In a later part of the section he returns to the same idea, saying of the followers of Lucretius and Pliny:

> They embrace and praise them, for the skilfullest and most excellent Philosophers that euer were, as having deliuered men from the greatest torments that could seize vpon them, and brought vnto them the greatest good that could befall them, by taking from them all feare of God, of hell, and of all punishment after this life.

But there is also a hint of Machiavellianism:

> If in outward shewe they professe religion, it is but to couer themselues vnder the vale thereof, to the end that men should not take them for such, as they are indeed, as also that they might keepe company with the best. But in their hearts, and amongst their companions they mocke and laugh at all religion.

Not the least interesting feature of the *French Academie* is the translator Thomas Bowes's Preface to the 1594 edition of the second part. Bowes considered it necessary to say something about atheism more applicable to his own day and nation than the remarks of the French writer of a generation before. For instance, he voices his apprehension that the atheism La Primaudaye had inveighed against in France had penetrated into England.

> And surely it is greatly to be feared that as their disguised attire couereth the bodies of many of our people and maketh them deformed, so this poison of Atheisme hath praised [*sic*] the narrow seas and is landed in the harts of no small number.

In 1557 La Primaudaye could only glance at Machiavellianism, but Bowes wished it to be known in 1594 that the students of the Florentine secretary were the very leaders of the atheists:

> In the forefront of which company, the students of Machiavels principles and practicers of his precepts may worthily bee raunged. This bad fellow whose works are no lesse accounted of among his followers . . . . then the sacred Scriptures are among sound Christians, blushed not to belch out these horrible blasphemies against pure religion, and so against God the Author thereof, namely, That the religion of the heathen made them stout and couragious, wheras Christian religion maketh the professors therof base minded, timorous, and fit to become a prey to everyone. These and such like positions [*sic*] are spued out by this hel hound.

When Bowes comes to give the names of the most famous atheists of all times, he shows himself familiar with the conventional list, pointing to Protagoras, Diagoras, Lucretius, and Pliny among the ancients, and among the moderns to Leo X, Rabelais, Jodelle, and Machiavelli, all of whom are represented as having died under the most horrible and shameful circumstances. Among the English none is mentioned by name, but there is a reference to Robert Greene so clear as to be unmistakable. The passage in Greene's *Repentance* where he had said that he did not fear to go to hell, since he would have there the company of better men than himself, is fully retold, and Bowes concludes, "The voice of a meere Atheist, and so afterwards he pronounced himselfe when he was checked in conscience by the mighty hand of God."

In the year 1587 the French Huguenot François de la Noue published at Paris his *Discours politiques et militaires*, the main purpose of which was to refute the *Discourses* of Machiavelli but which contained a great deal of practical information about the ordering of armies, and it was promptly translated into English by E. Aggas and published at London in 1588 with the title *Politike and Militarie Discovrses*. This contains several references to Epicures and atheists much in the tone of what we have heard before. In the twenty-fourth chapter, for instance, under the title "Against Those That Thinke That Godlinesse Depriueth Man of All Pleasures," La Noue tells us that France is overrun with an infinite number of Epicures. So numerous are they in fact that they can be divided into three classes: those of the court, the city, and the army. He then proceeds to summarize the opinions of each class, but they turn out to be all about the same, all holding that the chief end of life is pleasure and that there will be no future accounting for sins committed in this world.

It was also in 1587 that Arthur Golding completed the translation, begun by Sir Philip Sidney, of Philip Mornay's *De la verité de la religion chrestienne*, which had first appeared at Antwerp in 1581, and published it with the title *The Trewnesse of the Christian Religion: Against Atheists, Epicures, Paynims, Iewes, Mahumetists, and Other Infidels.* This great work, over six hundred pages in length, from the pen of the Huguenot statesman differs from the other treatments we have considered in its singleness of purpose and in the complete and sweeping nature of its denunciations. Others had touched on different points of the controversy, but Mornay touched them all, and in addition wrote with sincerity and conviction and with a wealth of learning that must have satisfied even Thomas Nashe, who had said that no one should undertake battle against atheism until he had run over infinite labyrinths of books and become familiar with the confessions of all philosophers.[7] In another respect also he satisfied Nashe's requirements, for he renounced the use of Scripture in his arguments and boldly met all adversaries on their own grounds, combating them either by reason or by their own authors.

A glance at his most important chapter headings will reveal how nearly Mornay came to covering the whole question of religious unbelief. He begins with a chapter in which he shows that there is a God, the proofs being the conventional ones of natural order, universal consent, the chain of being, and various refinements of these; chapter ii, "That There Is Only One God"; chapter v, "That in the One Essence of God There Are Three Persons"; chapter vii, "That the World Had a Beginning," written against Aristotle; chapter xi, "That God by His Providence Governeth the World," against the Epicures; chapter xiii, "That Mans Soule Is Immortall," in which no detail about the nature of the soul is omitted, its three powers, its ability to leave the body and exist independent of the senses, its desire for immortality, and the necessity for immortality if God is just, all being considered; chapter xxvi, "That the Things Which Seeme Most Wonderfull in Our Scriptures, Are Confirmed by the Heathen Themselves."

One special point of Mornay's work deserves consideration. Why did he consider it necessary to refute "Paynims, Iewes, and

[7] R. B. McKerrow, *Works of Thomas Nashe*, II, 125.

Mahumetists"? With the spread of the Turkish Empire in the Mediterranean and to the very gates of Vienna, Christianity found itself occupying a very small part of the habitable globe, and there may have been some apprehension as to whether or not it would be able to survive. There was thus a good deal of interest in the Mohammedans and their religion. But this was not the cause for Mornay's concern. He had been aroused by quite a different phase of the problem, and in my judgment this was nothing less than the rise, from a comparison of the different faiths, of a natural religion or deism. The entire classical revival, and especially the revival of Stoicism, were, as we have seen, a strong incitement to such a development, and that the movement was already under way in France by 1563 we have the word of Pierre Viret in his *Exposition de la doctrine de la foy chrestienne.* Only a few years after Mornay's work appeared, Jean Bodin in his *Colloquium Heptaplomeres* (1588) brought together seven representatives of the world's leading religions and allowed them to dispute freely on all points and thus to bring out the fact that there were certain fundamentals on which all could agree. Bodin, to be sure, nowhere mentions the word "deist" and indeed allows each of his characters to retain his own religion, but the implication is too clear to be mistaken, and for that reason the work was never published during his life.

But no long search into the thought of the time is needed to show that Mornay's book was in part directed against the deism that was developing from a comparison of religions. Mornay was certainly aware of the movement, although perhaps somewhat vaguely, and recognized in it a strong anti-Christian tendency. Indeed, apparently without even knowing the word "deism" he actually listed the main points of the belief. In his Preface to the reader immediately after a discussion of the Epicures he says:

Some goe yet a little further, both in respect of God and of themselues: They thinke there is a God, and that of him man hath receiued an immortall soule: that God gouerneth all things, and that man ought to serue him. But forasmuch as they see both Gentiles and Iewes, Turkes and Christians in the world, and in diuers nations diuers Religions, whereof euery one thinketh hee serueth God, and that he shall finde saluation in his owne Religion: These (like men at the stop where many wayes meet) in stead of chusing the right way by the iudgement of reason, doe stand still amazed, and in that amazement conclude that all comes to one.

Popular as La Primaudaye and Mornay were in England, they must yet yield first place to the Huguenot poet Guillaume du Bartas, the author of the poem *La semaine, ou création du monde,* which in the seven years after its first publication in 1578 went through twenty-eight separate editions in France. Although the complete edition of the *Divine Weeks,* as it came to be called, was not published in England until Joshua Sylvester's translation appeared in 1605, Du Bartas had been popular from the very first and various fragmentary translations had been licensed and published. The first to undertake the task of placing Du Bartas in English seems to have been Sir Philip Sidney, and in 1588 a *Translation of Salust du Bartas done by Sir Ph. Sidney* was licensed to W. Ponsonby but apparently not printed. In 1590 a fragment translated by Sylvester was printed, and in 1595–96 "The First Day of the First Week," also by Sylvester. During this time also there broke out with hardly a dissenting voice a full chorus of praise for the French poet that lasted until about the middle of the seventeenth century and then suddenly ceased, never to be resumed.

The modern student may well wonder how, at a time when Spenser and Shakespeare were writing, such wooden lines could have been called "sugar'd" and how such an interminable poem, much of it hardly more than biblical paraphrase, could ever have been read with any interest. That mystery is not likely ever to be completely dissipated, but we should remember, by way of partly understanding it, that much contemporary interest attached to a phase of the work likely to escape the notice of the modern reader. Du Bartas seems to have had as his main purpose in writing of the creation of the world a refutation of the current theories of the Aristotelians, who held that the world was eternal, and of the Epicureans, who said that it had been created by chance. The *Divine Weeks,* then, was by way of being not merely a tiresome elaboration of the biblical narrative

but a refutation of atheistical thought, and as such it was undoubtedly received and appreciated. Certainly the author lets
slip no opportunity to excoriate Epicurus, Aristotle, the Stoics,
atheists, Copernicus, and human learning in general. For the
refinements and subtleties of philosophic thought he has, to be
sure, very little respect. He states the opinions of the philosophers in the baldest, most straightforward way, stripped of
everything that might puzzle the simple, and this fact also may
not be without significance in an explanation of his enormous
popularity.

Let us glance briefly at the main points in rationalism and
atheism that Du Bartas saw fit to touch upon. In the first place,
he states unequivocally that he has no respect for the capacity
of the human mind and strongly implies that the power of reason and intellectual curiosity are devices of the devil. God, according to Du Bartas, meant for man only to believe the Bible:

> So do I more the sacred Tongue esteem . . . .
> Then all the golden Wit-pride of Humanity,
> Wherewith men burnish their erronious vanity.
> I'll rather give a thousand times the lie
> To mine owne Reason, then but once defie
> The sacred voice of th' everlasting Spirit.[8]

The first philosopher to be refuted is Aristotle, since it was he
who was most often cited as in conflict with the Bible story of
creation. It was Aristotle's opinion that nothing could be made
from nothing, but the Bible said that the world was so made.
No one could doubt where Du Bartas stood, although he was
willing to grant that when applied to matter *after* the creation
Aristotle's dictum was true:

> For, all that's made, is made of the *First Matter*
> Which in th' old *Nothing* made the All-Creator:
> All that dissolves, resolves into the same;
> Since first the Lord of nothing made This Frame,
> Nought's made of nought, and nothing turns to nothing.

Similarly Aristotle and the other Greeks are taken to task for
holding that the world was eternal, and later, during the dis-

[8] Grosart, *Complete Works of Joshua Sylvester*, p. 37.

cussion of the creation of Adam, for their theories of the universal soul.

Epicurus and his followers are condemned time and again
throughout the poem for their conception of a resting God who
exercises no providence over the world and for their theory of a
chance creation. Thus in "The Seventh Day of the First Week"
Du Bartas says:

> Fond *Epicure*, thou rather sleep'st, thy self,
> When thou did'st forge thee such a sleep-sick Elf
> For Life's pure fount; or vainly fraudulent
> (Not shunning th' Atheist's sin, but punishment)
> Imagined'st a God so perfect-less.

The arguments Du Bartas is able to muster against such theories
usually take a form similar to the following:

> The Lord our God wants neither Diligence,
> Nor Love, nor Care, nor Pow'r, nor Providence.

but occasionally he is willing to offer something a little more
convincing than an unsupported statement. While attempting
to establish the providence of God against those who had
pointed to the presence of so many savage animals in the world,
he says that the animals were tame enough in the Garden of
Eden and man has only himself to blame that they are savage
now. Then he declares that these animals actually serve a good
purpose by keeping men's wits sharp, that they are few in number, and that they have their natural enemies to prey upon
them.

Perhaps the most interesting single point in the whole poem
is Du Bartas's vigorous reaction to the new conception of the
universe developed by Copernicus and other students of astronomy. We have noticed very little of this in England, and
have not found that Copernicus was even known by name, but
Du Bartas seems to have been fairly familiar with what was
being discovered in the scientific world. In "The Fourth Day
of the First Week" he speaks of

> Those Clarks that think (think how absurd a jest)
> That neither Heav'ns nor Stars do turne at all,

> Nor dance about this great round Earthly Ball;
> But th' Earth itself, this massie Globe of ours,
> Turns round-about once every twice-twelve hours,

and goes on to argue that if this were so, an arrow shot straight up into the air would fall far to the westward of the shooter, and if a gun were shot toward the east, the bullet would never leave the barrel. And he concludes:

> Arm'd with these Reasons, 't were superfluous
> T'assaile the Reasons of *Copernicus;*
> Who, to salve better of the Stars th' appearance,
> Unto the Earth a three-fold motion warrants:
> Making the Sun the Center of this All,
> Moon, Earth, and Water, in one onely Ball.

Other works of considerable importance, such as Mornay's *Knowledge of a Mans Owne Selfe*, translated by Anthony Munday in 1602, might be mentioned, but the ones already reviewed are certainly sufficient to indicate the possibility of French sources for English thought about religious unbelief. Moreover, it should be remembered that although this chapter has dealt only with translated works, there were many others that never were put into English. By dealing only with translations I have of course not meant to imply that these others were not read in England or that they were not influential also.

IX

The Reaction
The Poets: Sir John Davies, John Davies of Hereford, Fulke Greville

WHENEVER a body of philosophic thought is endowed with enough vitality to appeal to the imagination, it sooner or later finds expression in poetry, and in this respect the reaction to atheism in the sixteenth century was no exception. We have traced the slow growth of this movement from a beginning sufficiently prosaic in 1530 and have observed how the denunciations, confutations, and reasoned refutations multiplied in number and how the ideas became more and more conventional in expression. We have observed also how the movement in France, where it had developed earlier, had already in 1578 called forth a poem from Du Bartas that had enjoyed an almost unparalleled popularity in England. And so it seems almost inevitable that in England at a time when poetry was the most popular form of literature the body of ideas that made up the reaction should eventually find themselves set forth in verse.

The three poets whose contributions we are to consider are Sir John Davies, John Davies of Hereford, and Fulke Greville, all of them minor figures in the history of literature but of enough force to impress themselves on their times, and one of them, Sir John Davies, to survive on his own merits as a poet. Professor E. H. Sneath, indeed, regards his *Nosce Teipsum* as one of the finest pieces of philosophical verse in the English language,[1] and although the other poems we are to study deserve no such en-

---

[1] *Philosophy in Poetry, a Study of Sir John Davies's Poem "Nosce Teipsum"* (New York, 1903), p. vii.

comiums, their authors were nevertheless not altogether inconsiderable as poets and thinkers and at least for our subject are of no small importance.

It was near the end of the year 1597 that John Davies, late of Oxford and a barrister in the Middle Temple, startled his mess companions by rushing into the hall where dinner was in progress armed with a dagger and accompanied by two attendants bearing swords. The meaning of this martial demonstration was immediately apparent. Davies set upon a fellow-commoner, Richard Martin, thrashed him severely, breaking a cudgel over his head, and then rushed to the door of the hall where he stopped long enough to wave a sword in the air. This was extraordinary conduct from a man who a year later was to be the author of one of the finest philosophical poems in the language, but it was not without its bearing on that event. In February of 1598 Davies was expelled from the Temple by unanimous sentence, and evidently at a loss for anything else to do with his enforced leisure he retired to Oxford for another year's study. Here, smarting under his punishment and no doubt suffering some remorse of conscience, he composed the poem *Nosce Teipsum*. In one place, while speaking of the lessons taught us by adversity, he refers to his own case in the following terms:

> This mistresse lately pluckt me by the eare,
> And many a golden lesson hath me taught;
> Hath made my Senses quicke, and Reason cleare,
> Reform'd my Will and rectifide my Thought.[2]

Davies divides his poem into two parts, "Of Humane Knowledge" and "Of the Soule of Man and the Immortalitie Thereof." The first of these, only a few pages in length, is on the dispraise of learning theme, which with Davies became the disparagement of all arts and sciences on the ground that since the fall of man and the darkening of his mind by sin only a few sparks of his former intellectual splendor have remained. How can one presume to any knowledge of the world, Davies asks, when he cannot render any judgment of the form and being of his own

---

[2] A. B. Grosart, *The Complete Poems of Sir John Davies*, I, 23.

soul? Nevertheless, made introspective by his affliction and seeking for illumination from above, he makes bold to undertake this difficult task of delineating the features of the soul.

Before discussion can proceed a definition must be agreed on. What is the soul? The wise men have never been able to give a satisfactory answer, Davies says:

> One thinks the Soule is aire; another, fire;
> Another blood, diffus'd about the heart;
> Another saith, the elements conspire,
> And to her essense each doth giue a part.
>
> Musicians thinke our Soules are harmonies,
> Phisicians hold that they complexions bee;
> Epicures make them swarmes of atomies,
> Which doe by chance into our bodies flee.[3]

Then, rejecting Aristotle and his definition of the soul as a quality and following Plato and the Christian writers, Davies defines it as a spiritual substance:

> The Soul a substance, and a spirit is,
> Which God Himselfe doth in the body make;
> Which makes the Man: for euery man from this;
> The nature of a Man, and name doth take.

He then advances arguments to show "that the soule is a thing subsisting by it selfe without the body," the object, of course, being to refute the Peripatetics, who had made the soul dependent on the senses and hence mortal. The proofs Davies brings are the time-honored ones that the soul can leave the body in imagination and that she has a power above that of the senses since she forms conclusions and generalizations from their reports and sometimes checks them and condemns what they prefer. If man had only sense, then the animals would outstrip him, for oftentimes their organs of sense are keener than his. And the matter is aptly summed up in two stanzas:

---

[3] *Ibid.*, pp. 26–27. Aristotle (*De anima* i. 2), Cicero (*Disputationes Tusculanae* i. 9–11), Nemesius (*De naturâ hominis* ii. 1), Lactantius (*De opificio dei* ii. 85), and Cornelius Agrippa (*De incertitudine scientiarum* lii) as well as many other writers on the subject had treated the matter of diversity of opinions in almost exactly the same way. Nemesius went into the matter at great length, giving a full chapter to the refutation of each false theory.

> But why doe I the Soule and Sense diuide?
> When Sense is but a power, which she extends;
> Which being in diuers parts diuersifide,
> The diuers formes of obiects apprehends?

> This power spreds outward, but the root doth grow
> In th' inward Soule, which onely doth perceiue;
> For th' eyes and eares no more their obiects know,
> Then glasses know what faces they receiue.[4]

After a detailed study of the various faculties and powers of the soul, Davies, in the last third of the poem, attempts to prove immortality and to answer the principal objections that have been urged against the idea. The Epicures have said that the soul grows old in the body and that it is corrupted in idiots, and have gone on to conclude that it is dependent on the bodily senses and so incapable of immortality. Here Davies merely repeats his earlier evidence for believing the soul to be superior to any bodily function, but when the Epicures wish to know why the dead do not return to tell us of their new abode, he comes forward with the novel idea that this would be as absurd as to expect a man to wish to return to his mother's womb after experiencing the freedom and joys of life in the world and says the very fact that the dead do not return is proof that they have found a happy resting place or else are imprisoned in hell. The final objection is a familiar one:

> Well, well, say these vaine spirits, though vain it is
> To thinke our Soules to Heauen or Hell do goe,
> Politike men haue thought it not amisse,
> To spread this lye, to make men vertuous so.[5]

This is briefly disposed of on the grounds that Calvin had taken,[6] that the desire for immortality is stamped on the hearts of all men, even the most savage, and is too universal to be a mere device of politicians. And Davies closes his proof with the striking analogy that as there are three powers in man—the vegetative, the sensitive, and the intellectual—so are there three stages in his life—prenatal existence, merely vegetative; life in this world,

4 Grosart, I, 39.

5 Grosart, I, 110.   6 *Institutes*, I, iii.

where the senses reach perfection and reason begins; and life in the world to come, where intellect will be supreme.

This summary is detailed enough to show how thoroughly Davies had mastered his sources and how completely he had oriented himself in a certain current of thought. He wrote with a background of enormous richness and extent and expressed hardly an idea that cannot be pointed out in the works of dozens of his predecessors. Indeed, parallels close enough to convince the unwary of indebtedness may be drawn up between *Nosce Teipsum* and the works of Aristotle, Cicero, Nemesius, Lactantius, Augustine, Cornelius Agrippa, Calvin, Bullinger, Melanchthon, Viret, La Primaudaye, Mornay, Rastell, and Woolton, and probably of others whom my reading has not included. *Nosce Teipsum* is an admirable poem and reveals its author as a man of vigorous and active mind, but the body of thought with which it deals was so familiar to educated men of the time that no doubt most of them never stopped to consider whence it was derived.

Notwithstanding these facts, there have not been lacking writers to make very positive assertions about Davies' indebtedness to particular works. The first of these seems to have been the eighteenth-century hydrographer Alexander Dalrymple, who wrote, "Sir John Davies' poem on the Immortality of the soul is chiefly taken from Nemesius' *De natura hominis*."[7] Grosart indignantly repudiated this statement, more, it seems, with the naïve idea of defending our author from the charge of "plagiarism" than of discovering the truth, and declared the poem to be one of "deep and original thought" and Davies indebted to no one.[8] But the idea could not be laid by mere indignant denial. Professor E. H. Sneath in his careful study of the poem found Davies to have drawn his ideas from Aristotle, Cicero, Nemesius, and Calvin, and some years later Margarete Seeman was able to substantiate his findings as far as Aristotle

[7] Quoted by John Nichols in his *Illustrations of the Literary History of the Eighteenth Century* (London, 1822), IV, 549–50.

[8] Memorial-Introduction to *op. cit.*, p. lxi.

was concerned by numerous parallel passages between *De anima* and *Nosce Teipsum*. Better equipped for the task than any of these was Professor Louis I. Bredvold, who argued convincingly that the psychological ideas in the poem had been taken from La Primaudaye's *French Academie*,[9] and thus far his position has not been successfully assailed. It was not to refute but rather to supplement Professor Bredvold's work that some years ago I undertook to prove,[10] by means of verbal similarities and two or three ideas common to the authors in question that I could find in no earlier writer, that for his proofs of immortality Davies had drawn rather heavily on Philip Mornay's *Trunesse of the Christian Religion*.

Thus the matter stands at present, and with the exception of one rather elementary observation I have nothing further to add. No one will doubt, I suppose, that Aristotle was the ultimate source for a number of ideas in *Nosce Teipsum*, just as no one will question that about nine-tenths of the body of Renaissance thought was originally worked out in ancient Greece. But it is contrary to everything we have learned about the spread of ideas to suppose that any great part of English thought in the sixteenth century was drawn directly from the Greek masters, and certainly before concluding that any work was thus derived the student should investigate thoroughly the literature of Renaissance France and Italy. In so doing Professor Bredvold and I have employed sounder methods than Sneath and Seeman, and have reached, I think, sounder conclusions.

A few years after the appearance of *Nosce Teipsum* an ingenious master of penmanship, also named John Davies but called John Davies of Hereford to distinguish him from Sir John, began to turn his talent to verse of a philosophical kind and to grace his rather mediocre efforts with elaborate editions introduced by laudatory sonnets to the important noblemen of

---

[9] "The Sources Used by Davies in *Nosce Teipsum*," *Publications of the Modern Language Association*, XXXVIII (1923), 745-69.

[10] "The Indebtedness of *Nosce Teipsum* to Mornay's *Trunesse of the Christian Religion*," *Modern Philology*, XXV (1927), 67-78.

England. In 1603 appeared his *Microcosmos*, which, as its name indicates, is a discussion of the soul and all its faculties, each of the passions and examples of their working, the three souls of man as conceived by Aristotle, and all the other conventional material of such works. There are in addition, however, several excursions into other fields, a history of England, and a long section on princely policy, in the contra-Machiavellian tradition, for the benefit of James I.

Near the end of the poem the resemblance to *Nosce Teipsum* becomes even greater. Davies of Hereford, like Sir John, reviews the opinions of the ancient philosophers about the nature of the soul and its location in the body and passes on to refute various false theories about its origin, that souls are engendered by parents or stored up in heaven, of course concluding himself that they are created separately by God and sent into the body before birth. Like all the other Christian apologists, he defines the soul as a substance, affirms that it is bodiless, and comments on its ability to leave the body in thought or in dreams. Thus he comes inevitably to the proofs for immortality. We are first told that the very doubts and disputations concerning immortality are an evidence for it,

> What soule can doubt her immortality,
> But such as is immortal?[11]

and that further evidence is the universal desire for immortality, the change observed in those who have denied it as they approach death, and the fact that the soul does not depend on the senses and often concludes contrary to their reports.

Unfortunately for our inquiry, with the exception of a worthless reference to "damned Epicurean-Libertines" Davies of Hereford supplies us with no information about the men of his own day who were denying immortality. In an earlier work, *Mirum in modum* (1602), he had seemed to affirm that there were atheists abroad,

> But with what words can I their blame bewray,
> That maugre all that euer can be saide,

---

[11] Grosart, *Complete Works of John Davies of Hereford*, I, 86.

> To proue this God; will all that All gainesay,
> And flat affirme, and speake as well apaide,
> *There is no God,*

and in the same work had devoted fifty-four stanzas to demonstrating God's providence against the Lucretians. But when he finally comes to naming the atheists, the only ones he can think of are Pherecides the Assyrian, Pyrrho, Justinian, Lucian, and Alphonso X of Spain.

A consideration of Fulke Greville's *Treatise of Humane Learning*[12] has been deferred to the last for two reasons. First, the date is doubtful. The poem was never printed until the 1633 edition of Greville's collected works, where we are told on the title-page that it was written "in his youth and familiar exercise with Sir Philip Sidney." There seems to be no particular reason to distrust this, although it must be remembered that publishers were only too ready to trade on the name of Sidney. Second, the *Treatise* is the first work we have studied that is devoted entirely to the dispraise of learning,[13] and as such it opens up for us a new field of inquiry.

Before any progress can be made in this new direction a summary of the poem seems necessary. Greville begins by deploring man's thirst for knowledge, since it is a desire that can never be fulfilled in this world and since because of it man ate of the forbidden fruit and lost his immortal heritage. Knowledge is impossible in the first place because the senses, the only organs through which knowledge can come, are imperfect, fallible, and variable. Next, the imagination, which receives the reports of the senses, is not only misled by their false intelligence, but in itself is imperfect, subject to the affections and prone to the creation of dreams and apparitions. Again, the memory, the register of sense, is too notoriously faulty to need any comment, and even the understanding, the chief oracle of what man knows, re-

---

[12] On the title-page it is written *Treatie,* but I suppose this to be a misprint for *Treatise.* As usual, I have used Grosart's reprint.

[13] The introductory stanzas of *Nosce Teipsum* had touched on this subject, but *Nosce Teipsum* is essentially a poem about immortality and is thus aligned with another tradition.

tains only a few faint perceptions of general truths and is so corrupted by ignorance and sin as to be unworthy of any credence.

Perhaps, then, arts and sciences can supply these natural defects in man and help him to a position of intellectual self-re-
spect. Not in Greville's opinion. This high-praised learning is
nothing but word magic, and philosophy is but books of poetry
compiled in prose. It is condemned in God's word as a vain de-
ceit, and the Lacedemonians did well when they scorned it as
idle and effeminate and the Romans when they drove the Greek
teachers from their walls like Turks. Indeed, how can these arts
pretend to any truth when they are all founded on the knowledge of evil, all the fruit of our original sin, and when man himself and the world and all it contains are still under the primal
curse?

> Againe, if all man's fleshly organs rest
>   Vnder that curse, as out of doubt they doe;
> If skie, sea, Earth, lye vnder it opprest,
>   As tainted with that taste of error too;
> In this mortalitie, this strange priuation,
> What knowledge stands but sense of declination?

We are not on these accounts utterly to condemn learning,
however. We should choose and read with care and remember
that learning is a bunch of grapes sprung up among thorns which
none can hope to pluck without harm unless great caution is
used. But before giving any precepts for the use or reform of
human arts Greville first excludes from his discussion the meek
and humble children of God, who, in the world but not of it,
have chosen the wisest part of all. He then proceeds to explain,
in nearly a hundred stanzas, that all learning should be radically
reformed, that superfluous and curious arts should be lopped
off, that no bookish science, nothing not drawn from nature,
should be tolerated, that life and action ought to be the immediate aims of all instruction. Practical use must govern all. Eloquence, for instance, is not to insinuate and persuade but to
state plainly what things are in nature; arithmetic, geometry,
and astronomy are not to lose themselves in idle theories but to
apply themselves to trade and navigation. Finally, this discus-

sion finished, Greville returns to the wisely ignorant children of
God,

> Who, in the wombe of God's true Church, their mother,
> Learne they that know Him well, must know no other,

and devotes a section to their praise for having renounced these
vanities of human learning.

Now it is clear enough that Greville's poem is not so direct a
reaction to rationalistic thought as most of the other works we
have studied, but that it is one seems to me beyond question.
The passage just quoted, "they that know Him well, must know
no other," is the keynote of the poem. Philosophy, metaphys-
ics, thought for its own sake, any sort of learning except the
most practical and matter of fact, Greville would banish, not
only because such learning is useless, but because it is godless
as well. The higher branches are calculated only to lead men
away from God and fix their minds on the follies of this world.
But farther than this in determining the nature of his reaction
it seems impossible to go, for no atheists and no particular group
of unbelievers are mentioned. At times, indeed, it appears that
Greville is merely condemning the "Schoolmen's sleepy speculations" or any other abstract learning, but of course he may have
had vaguely in mind the irreligious tendencies of Aristotelian
learning, or, somewhat more likely, I think, the dangerous direction taken by the natural sciences under Copernicus, Cardan,
and Bruno. It was probably this last to which he was referring
when, in the course of his warnings to all who pursue knowledge,
he said:

> Next that we doe not ouerbuild our states,
> In searching secrets of the Deity,
> Obscurities of Nature, casualtie of fates;
> But measure first our own humanity.

An eccentricity of scholarship only partly explainable by the
difference in the literary merit of the two works is that the background and possible sources of *Nosce Teipsum* have been studied
with great care and that the *Treatise of Humane Learning* has
thus far completely escaped any such attention. Yet the latter
poem, if without quite so many literary antecedents, has a background of great antiquity and extent, and one of perhaps even

more interest than that of *Nosce Teipsum* because of its greater
complexity and because it is ornamented by Renaissance figures
of no less importance than Montaigne and Sir Walter Raleigh.
The first part of the poem, the denial of the validity of sensory
impression and the belief that, misled by the senses and impo-
tent in itself, the human mind is incapable of knowing the
truth, has for its ultimate source the thought of the Greek sage
Pyrrho as it was set down and elaborated by his most famous
disciple, Sextus Empiricus, in the *Pyrrhonean Hypotyposes* or
Pyrrhonic Sketches. It was the contention of the Pyrrhonists
that since there is no statement that cannot be refuted, since the
senses cannot be trusted, seeing that they vary between man
and animals, among men themselves, and in individual men at
different periods of life and states of health, the only position
for a reasonable man to take is one of complete suspension of
judgment. The followers of Pyrrho were never to state a decided opinion but to preface or conclude all their utterances with
the formulas "Nothing more," or "I decide nothing," or "All is
false." Thus their position was one of pure skepticism, although
they did not, like the Academicians, declare the truth both unknown and unknowable, but represented themselves as still
seeking.

Although frequently condemned by the clergy as inimical to
Christianity, Pyrrhonism, along with Stoicism and Epicureanism, was revived during the Renaissance, especially in France,
and enjoyed a good deal of popularity. This revival probably
began as a part of the general enthusiasm for Cicero, for the
Pyrrhonism prevalent in the early part of the Renaissance seems
to have stemmed from Cicero's *Academic Questions* rather than
from the works of Sextus Empiricus, but the movement soon
accommodated itself to a phase of Renaissance thought then
just beginning to develop. The closed systems of the Middle
Ages had broken down and mental horizons had suddenly broadened in two directions, backward into classical antiquity and
outward into the newly discovered lands across the seas, in both
directions including varieties of men, customs, and religions
hitherto shut out from the narrow systems of thought. It was

the revelation of this infinite variety of men and beliefs that shocked the more active minds of Europe out of their complacency and rendered them critical of their own creeds and even of their own mental habits. To this state of mind Pyrrhonism easily adjusted itself, for it was a philosophy that built on the variety that had so impressed the men of the Renaissance and concluded from it that the truth is still unknown.

Literary evidences of the movement are plentiful. In 1527 Henry Cornelius Agrippa of Nettesheim published at Cologne his *De incertitudine scientiarum*, in which, founding himself upon the Academicians and the Pyrrhonists, he undertook to display, in a half-bantering, half-serious tone, the vanities of all branches of learning. In 1538 Sadolet in his *Phaedrus* and in 1546 Saint-Gelais in *Advertissement sur les jugements d'astrologie* attacked the Pyrrhonists, as did Rabelais in the third book of *Pantagruel*, thus giving evidence of the importance the current of thought was assuming. The system was not without an important defense during this period, however, for Omer Talon in *Academia* (1548), after justifying his friend Ramus for his attack on Aristotle, passed on and stated his philosophical purpose to be "to deliver opinionated men, enslaved by fixed philosophical beliefs and reduced to a shameful servitude, to make them understand that true philosophy approaches things freely and openly and is not enchained to one opinion or to one author."[14] Talon founded his work in the main on Cicero's *Academic Questions*, and he assents to the position taken by the New Academy, which had argued both sides of all obscure questions and not taken the opinion of any philosopher or held continually by any one school. Again, Guy de Bruès in his *Dialogues contre les noveau academiciens* (1558) attacks the Pyrrhonists, but allows Baïf, a character in the dialogue, to state their opinions with a good deal of fidelity:

I see much that appears probable to me, but nothing of which I am sure.

I hold that there is no certainty in philosophy and the other disciplines and that all is only opinion and deceitful appearances.

All the things which we apprehend by the senses are false,[15]

[14] Translated from the citation of Henri Busson, *op. cit.*, p. 262.   [15] *Ibid.*, p. 422.

and also to ridicule the dialectics of the Schoolmen, geometry, arithmetic, astronomy, and astrology.

Thus far the current of Pyrrhonism had derived mainly from Cicero and the New Academy, but when in 1562 Henri Etienne published his Latin translation of the *Pyrrhonic Sketches* of Sextus Empiricus, the movement was given a good deal of impetus. It was no doubt this edition as well as some of the other works we have listed that Montaigne used in his *Apology for Raymond Sebond* (1580), one of the finest summaries not only of Pyrrhonism but of skeptical thought in general that the century affords, and it was more than likely this edition also from which Sir Walter Raleigh in his *Sceptic* translated into English the first three Pyrrhonic tropes.

How, it may be inquired, did Christianity succeed in turning Pyrrhonism to its own purposes? It would seem that a system that had been able to absorb Aristotle with only a few pangs of indigestion would encounter little difficulty here, but the fact is that it did not always succeed to its own satisfaction, and was more than a little apprehensive. There was always the danger that a philosophy which declared everything else to be uncertain and a matter of opinion would not exclude Christianity from that general conclusion, and this, in fact, is the step that Montaigne more than once very nearly takes. But Christianity, recognizing its ally in a potential enemy, declared the attitude of the Pyrrhonists justified by the doctrine of original sin[16] and with admirable promptness turned the weapons of Pyrrhonism against human learning, always, in some form or other, the enemy of Christianity. This is exactly what Greville did, as Cornelius Agrippa had done before him, and thus his reason for so carefully exempting God's pure children from the application of his remarks is easy to understand. Pyrrhonism was a sword that would cut both ways, and the easiest thing was merely to declare the Christians out of its reach.

There is no doubt that the background we have hastily sketched in is the one against which Greville was writing, but to

---

[16] As we have noticed in both *Nosce Teipsum* and the *Treatise of Humane Learning*.

go farther and identify the particular work upon which he drew is a much more difficult task. We are not to fall into the error of supposing that because the *Treatise of Humane Learning* is in the Pyrrhonic tradition Greville used or had even read the *Pyrrhonean Hypotyposes*. If he had any one source it is to be searched for among his Renaissance predecessers, who had given the new direction to the Pyrrhonic current, and among these the most likely candidate appears to be Cornelius Agrippa. His *De incertitudine scientiarum* had been translated into English by James Sanford in 1568[17] and was the only one of the works we have mentioned available to Greville in English translation. Now the principal difference between the works of Agrippa and Greville is one of tone. Agrippa, like Erasmus in the *Praise of Folly*, was not very serious and assumed the bantering, scoffing air that characterized the attitude of the Humanists toward the abuses of their day, while the seriousness of Greville's poem is without relief.

Yet in subject matter the similarities between the two works are rather striking. In his first chapter Agrippa said, "If we may be bold to confess the Truth, the Traditions of all sciences are so dangerous and inconstant, that it is far safer to be Ignorant, than to know," and this is very nearly the text of the *Treatise of Humane Learning*. Moreover, Agrippa attacked physics, geometry, arithmetic, astronomy, and all the other sciences that Greville condemned, and in addition made a special point of displaying the follies and stupidities of the Schoolmen. Agrippa, of course, wrote with the university struggle of the Greeks and Trojans still fresh in mind, but that Greville should return to this theme when there was so little in his own day to justify it would seem to argue that he was following a much earlier work. Finally, in his concluding chapter Agrippa, like Greville was later to do, returns to the lowly followers of Christ and praises them for renouncing the traditions of men and drawing their wisdom from an incorruptible source above.

17 Re-edited in 1575. I have used the London edition of 1684.

X

The Atheism of Christopher Marlowe

ONE of the most involved and baffling problems in the whole course of sixteenth-century literature, and one upon which many scholars have exercised the full force of their ingenuity, is the problem of Christopher Marlowe's atheism. The complexity of the matter grows out of the nature of the accusations made against Marlowe, by a man under arrest (Thomas Kyd) whom Marlowe may have betrayed, and by a government spy (Richard Baines), out of the fact that Marlowe himself was a government spy who was evidently playing some kind of very deep game, and out of the fact that according to the reports his atheism was connected with a seditious plot or libel against the state. Much light has been shed on the whole problem, it is true, by the researches of F. S. Boas,[1] Leslie Hotson,[2] S. A. Tannenbaum,[3] F. K. Brown,[4] and W. D. Briggs,[5] but the work of these has been mainly concerned with discovering the details of Marlowe's death and following up the careers of his associates. They have been concerned of course with whatever the records would reveal, but even the newly discovered documents have added very little to what we already know

[1] *The Works of Thomas Kyd* (Oxford, 1901), Introd., pp. i–cxvi, and *Fortnightly Review*, February, 1899, pp. 212–25.

[2] *The Death of Christopher Marlowe* (Harvard University Press, 1925).

[3] *The Assassination of Christopher Marlowe* (New York, 1928) and *The Booke of Sir Thomas Moore* (New York, 1927).

[4] *London Times Literary Supplement*, June 2, 1921.

[5] "On a Document concerning Christopher Marlowe," *Studies in Philology*, XX (1923), 153–59.

about Marlowe's atheism, and concerning the nature and origin of his unbelief, the matter of first importance for this study, we know not much more than we did when we began.

The story of Kyd's arrest, his implication of Marlowe in the charges of sedition and atheism, and of Marlowe's death has been many times retold.[6] But since the charge of atheism is almost inextricably connected with the other events of the plot and cannot be fully understood independent of them, it seems necessary to review the main points of the story here, although as briefly as coherence will allow.

On May 11, 1593, the Privy Council issued an order to a commission to arrest and search the premises of anyone suspected of setting up "diuers lewd and mutinous libells" within the city of London. One of the libels in particular is mentioned as being placed "uppon the wal of the Dutch Churchyard that doth exceed the rest of lewdness."[7] Any person suspected who refused to confess was to be put to the torture. The next day, May 12, Thomas Kyd was arrested, thrown in prison, and tortured in an effort either to make him confess or to force him to implicate others.

Thus at the beginning it seems clear that the Council was proceeding only against a plot or seditious mutiny. What the exact nature of this sedition really was has never been fully determined, but Boas and Tannenbaum, who have investigated the whole matter minutely, unite in the opinion that it had to do with the Flemish colony in London. Boas[8] points out that libels are known to have been set up against these people in April of that year and that in March there had been a bill introduced into the House of Commons to prevent them from selling foreign commodities at retail in England. The Privy Council feared that an uprising of the populace or at least of the apprentices would result, and that it would be followed by possible inter-

---

[6] Perhaps best by Boas and Hotson in the works just cited.

[7] The entire order is reprinted by Boas in *The Works of Thomas Kyd*, p. lxvii.

[8] *Ibid.*, p. lxviii.

national difficulties. Consequently they were anxious to stop the matter at once. One of the libels set up was in verse and began:

> You strangers, that inhabit in this land,
> Note this same writing, do it understand;
> Conceive it well, for safe-guard of your lives,
> Your goods, your children, and your dearest wives.

Dr. Tannenbaum accepts Boas' explanation but makes a much fuller use of the material by connecting the suppressed play *Sir Thomas Moore* with it. It is his opinion that Kyd, Mundy, Chettle, Dekker, and one or two other dramatists were writing this play for the definite purpose of causing an uprising in London against the foreigners, and that Marlowe, the government spy, revealed Kyd's part in it to the Privy Council. Hence the immediate arrest of Kyd and hence Kyd's attempt to retaliate upon Marlowe with every weapon at his command.

But the important feature of the affair for our purpose came apparently as an accident of Kyd's arrest, for while searching his premises, according to their order, the commission came upon a document that they declared atheistical. Kyd denied ownership of the document and said it belonged to Marlowe. In his letter to Lord Keeper Puckering, written, however, after Marlowe's death, he says:

When I was first suspected of that libell that concerned the state, amongst those waste and idle papers (which I carde not for) & which vnaskt I did deliuer vp, were founde some fragments of a disputation, toching that opinion, affirmed by Marlowe to be his, and shufled with some of myne (vnknown to me) by some occasion of or wrytinge in one chamber twoe yeares synce.[9]

The document in question, which fortunately has come down to us, is a fragment of a letter written by someone suspected of heresy to a church official, no doubt his bishop. Concerning it Mr. Boas says, "An examination of the contents proves that, so far from Atheistic, it is a methodical defense, based on scriptural texts, of Theistic or Unitarian doctrines."[10] So far as I

---

[9] Reprinted by S. A. Tannenbaum in his *The Booke of Sir Thomas Moore*, Appen. C, p. 108. F. S. Boas also reprints it in the Introduction to his *Works of Thomas Kyd*.

[10] *Works of Thomas Kyd*, p. lxx.

am aware, no documents that we today should call atheistic
(Mr. Boas is clearly using the word in its modern sense) have
ever been discovered in the sixteenth century, but it is a mistake to attempt to make this one appear harmless. The most
important paragraph in the fragment runs as follows:

> It is lawfull by many wayes to se the infirmitie of Jhesus Christ whom Paul
> in the last chapter to the Corinthians of the second Epistle denieth not to be
> crucified through infirmitie. And the whole course & consent of the Euangeli-
> call history doth make him subject to the passions of man as hunger thirst
> weariness & fear. To the same end ar swete anxietie continuall praier the con-
> solation of the Angell again spitting whipping rebukes or checks His corps
> wrapt in the linnen cloth vnburied And to beleue forsooth that this nature
> subject to theis infirmities & passions is God or any part of the diuine essence
> what is it other but to make God mightie & of power of thone part weak &
> impotent of thother part which thing to think wer madness & follie To per-
> suade others impieties.[11]

Thus the paper is a reasoned defense of the opinion that Jesus
Christ was only a human being, subject to human error, that he
was not a divinity, and that it was impiety to teach that he was.
Any such assertions could, and frequently did, send a man to the
stake. Already at Norwich, in Norfolk, five men had suffered
death by fire for similar opinions, opinions not at all more
heretical, the last of whom had been Francis Kett in 1589. Kyd
undoubtedly knew this, and hence his frantic disavowal of
ownership of the document and his efforts to clear himself of
even the shadow of suspicion.

It will be noted that, in attributing the fragment to Marlowe,
Kyd used the ambiguous expression "affirmed by Marlowe to
be his." Did he mean that Marlowe wrote it or only owned it?
His language was probably purposely ambiguous, for Dr. Tannenbaum has shown by careful comparison of handwriting[12]
that whoever owned or wrote it Thomas Kyd himself had
transcribed it. At this point the name of Francis Kett has been
obtruded into the problem as the possible author of the docu-

---

[11] Tannenbaum, *The Booke of Sir Thomas Moore*, pp. 103–4. Boas and Briggs (*loc. cit.*) have also reprinted the fragment.

[12] *The Booke of Sir Thomas Moore*, pp. 43–47.

ment. He was brought into it, however, on the sole ground that in his confession at Norwich he showed himself to hold similar Unitarian principles to those set forth in the Kyd paper, and because there was a chance that he could have known Marlowe at Cambridge or in London. Kett has been mentioned so often and with so much assurance by Grosart, Boas, and others that many students have received the impression that he figured largely in the charges against Marlowe, Raleigh, and Kyd. Actually there is not a scrap of evidence to connect him with Marlowe or any of his group, and thanks to the work of Mr. W. D. Briggs[13] his name has been removed from any direct connection with the controversy.

Briggs has shown that the fragment Kyd said was Marlowe's was really in existence as early as 1549. In that year John Proctor published a work entitled *The Fal of the Late Arrian* in which the document in question is attributed to "the late Arrian" and is reprinted and refuted section by section. When the refutation material is removed and the sections or paragraphs are all put together, they form exactly the same work as the one found in Kyd's study. In Kyd's copy the paragraphs are arranged somewhat differently, but there is no doubt whatever that it is the same work, and thus there is no doubt that Francis Kett could not have written it.

To return to the sequence of events. On May 18, probably on the basis of information furnished by Kyd, the Privy Council issued a warrant for the arrest of Christopher Marlowe, and that it was carried out is evident from an entry in the *Register of the Privy Council* for May 20:

This day Ch. Marley of London, gent., being sent for by warrant from their Lordships, hath entered his appearance accordinglie for his indemnity therein, and is commanded to give his dailie attandance on their Lordships till he shall be licensed to the contrairie.[14]

What the charge was is not stated, but if Kyd's oral accusation was anything like the two letters that he wrote to members of

---

[13] *Op. cit.*   [14] Boas, *The Works of Thomas Kyd*, p. lxii.

the Council after Marlowe's death,[15] it must have been for atheism or sedition or both.

It seems strange that a man with charges of such gravity hanging over him should have been allowed his freedom without bond on the easy condition that he report to the court once a day during its pleasure. But the explanation may not be very far to seek. In the first place, it should be noted that Marlowe was no stranger to the Privy Council. On June 29, 1587, after Cambridge had refused to grant him the M.A. degree, the Council sent down a letter that amounted to an arbitrary order that the degree be conferred. On the basis of this order and some other material Mr. Austin K. Gray has shown,[16] I think conclusively, that in the early part of 1587 Marlowe was a secret agent in the employment of the Privy Council. In fact, the order alone, with Mr. Gray's italics, seems to me sufficient to remove any doubt on the subject:

Whereas *it was reported that Christopher Morley was determined to have gone beyond the seas to Reames and there to remaine;* their lordships thought good to certifie that *he had no such intent;* but that in all his actions *he had behaved him selfe orderlie and discreetlie,* wherebie *he had done her Majestie good service* and deserved to be rewarded for his faithfull dealinge: their Lordships request was *that the rumor thereof should be allied by all possible meanes,* and that he should be furthered in the degree he was to take next Commencement: Because it was not her Majesties pleasure *that anie one emploid as he had been in matters touching the benefitt of the countrie* should be *defamed by those that are ignorant in th' affaires he went about.*[17]

[15] I.e., the letter to Lord Keeper Puckering (reprinted by Boas and Tannenbaum) and the letter to some other lord of the Council lately discovered and described by Brown (*op. cit.*) and carefully reprinted by W. W. Greg in *Literary Autographs* (Oxford University Press, 1925), No. XV.

[16] "Some Observations on Christopher Marlowe, Government Agent," *Publications of the Modern Language Association,* XLIII (1928), 682–700.

[17] Mr. Gray explains that the University of Douai at Rheims was the center of practically all the Catholic plots against England during this period. Many Catholic students from Cambridge went there to complete their work when about ready for the M.A. at Cambridge, and when the Cambridge authorities heard that Marlowe had gone there, they supposed he had turned Catholic and refused to grant him the degree. He possibly did go to Rheims as a spy on the Catholics. The Privy Council possibly meant he had no intention of remaining there, but the main thing for them was that the degree should be granted and all talk about the matter stopped forthwith.

Moreover, according to the Middlesex Session Roll, XXXI Elizabeth, October, 1588, Marlowe had been arrested before and two citizens had gone his bond for his appearance in court. Then also, as in May, 1593, the charges had been unstated, but it is not unreasonable to suppose that someone in Kyd's predicament had retaliated on him, and if so he must have been unable to sustain his accusations, for nothing more is heard of the matter.

If it is true, then, that it was Marlowe who betrayed Kyd to the Council, and the prompt arrest of Kyd after the issuance of the order points to the possession of secret information by the Council, the members of the Council would be inclined to discount Kyd's charges against Marlowe on the grounds that they were perhaps prompted by revenge. On the other hand, they may have thought it prudent to keep their eyes on Marlowe for a while, for they had already had experience with gentlemen in the espionage branch who knew how to play a double game.[18] But however it was, Marlowe had only a short respite. On May 29 a certain Richard Baines, another spy, hanged the following year, turned in to the Privy Council a "Note Containing the opinion of one Christopher Marley Concerning his damnable Judgment of Religion, and scorn of gods word." Here Marlowe is charged with lewd, almost unprintable blasphemies, with favoring Catholics, with holding and teaching atheism, and with the intention of counterfeiting the coin of the realm with the help of a Newgate prisoner.

What the action of the Council was or would have been on the receipt of this new information from a source apparently not under suspicion of personal motives we do not know. For the following day, May 30, Marlowe was killed in a tavern at Deptford under circumstances which even the brilliant work of Leslie Hotson and S. A. Tannenbaum has not altogether cleared up. Mr. Hotson has discovered the coroner's report of the inquest,

[18] Notably with Cholmeley, who was accused of allowing Catholics he had detected to escape for money. Mr. Conyers Read in his book *Sir Francis Walsingham* (Harvard University Press, 1925) has a good chapter, "Plots and Counterplots," on the many plots of the period and the part spies played in them.

held on June 1, and by it the name of the actual slayer, Ingram
Frizer, who swore that he struck in self-defense and only after
Marlowe had wounded him twice in the head. He was pardoned
by the Queen on June 28. Mr. Tannenbaum, seeking to penetrate deeper into the maze of plot, espial, and violence that surrounded the lives of Marlowe and his associates, has reached the
rather remarkable conclusion that Sir Walter Raleigh had him
killed.[19] Sir Walter, says Mr. Tannenbaum, knowing of the
Baines note, feared that Marlowe would be put to the torture
and would reveal the plot to raise the citizenry of London
against the Flemings and Sir Walter's atheism as well. So to
prevent any such untoward events he sent three of his men to
kill Marlowe at Deptford.

Very little actually came of all this stir about atheism, although Marlowe was remembered by several pious writers for
many years, by Thomas Beard in his *Theatre of Gods Judgements*
(1597) and by William Vaughan in his *Golden Grove* (1600).
Kyd's letters to members of the Privy Council probably cleared
him of the stigma, at least sufficiently for him to be released
from prison. He died the following year (1594), but whether his
torture and other prison experiences had anything to do with
his early death is only to be conjectured. Cholmeley, the man
whom Marlowe was said to have seduced to atheism, was arrested June 29, 1593, and imprisoned. A warrant had been out
for him, however, since March 19, perhaps for betrayal of trust,
as he had been a double-dealing spy. When he was finally arrested, he told bystanders not to worry about him as he would be
able to shift for himself, and he probably did, for at that point
he is lost sight of and has never since reappeared.

[19] In his *Assassination of Christopher Marlowe*, the greater part of the book being
given over to that thesis. I do not think it can be sustained. In the first place, it is
mere supposition, based on evidence of the most unconvincing and tenuous kind. Second, the Commission at Cerne Abbas the following year, appointed especially to investigate atheism, pursued its inquiries with great diligence but failed to uncover the
slightest scrap of actionable evidence against Sir Walter. Third, there were other spies
in the employment of the Council as able to reveal Sir Walter's complicity in a plot to
raise a London mob against the Flemings as Marlowe was, but we hear nothing more of
the matter.

The effort may now be made to inquire a little more closely into the nature of Marlowe's atheism and its possible sources, and this also is likely to prove a task of considerable difficulty. Marlowe was in many respects almost an epitome of his age. He had a full share of the Renaissance exuberance of spirit and love of action and was abreast of the thought of his time, but he was also a university man and familiar with the classics. All the currents of thought that made for religious unbelief seem to have combined in him to produce one of the best examples of what is well called Renaissance paganism. His atheism, if such it was, seems not to have been an organized philosophical system, but a temper of mind that expressed itself in life and action, quite unlike the objective, detached state of mind, having little relation to action, with which we are so familiar in the twentieth century. Now the difficulties in the way of analyzing the religious and philosophical opinions of a man who perhaps himself was unable to analyze them are obvious, and the following remarks must therefore be considered as only suggestive and not conclusive.

I think we may be fairly sure, nevertheless, that one of the influences most responsible for Marlowe's incredulity was Machiavellianism. Marlowe had entered Cambridge in 1581, at a time when, according to Harvey, the Florentine was enjoying a great vogue there and no doubt became one of the "odd crewe or tooe" that Harvey said had become "prettily well acquaynted with a certayne parlous booke called, as I remember me, Il Principe di Niccolo Machiavelli." Indeed his Machiavellianism is very well attested by the famous passage in Greene's *Groats-Worth of Wit*, already quoted in chapter vii.

Moreover, Marlowe's works themselves are sufficient evidence of the impression the thought of Machiavelli had made on him. In the *Jew of Malta*, for instance, Barabas at the beginning of the play declares that he is Machiavelli and testifies to the popularity of the Florentine's works in England:

> Albeit the world think Machiavel is dead,
> Yet was his soul but flown beyond the Alps;

> And, now the Guise is dead, is come from France,
> To view this land, and frolic with his friends.
> To some perhaps my name is odious;
> But such as love me, guard me from their tongues,
> And let them know that I am Machiavel,
> And weigh not men, and therefore not men's words. . . . .
> I count religion but a childish toy,
> And hold there is no sin but ignorance.[20]

The Guise here referred to is the Duke of Guise who figures largely in the *Massacre at Paris*. In this play the Duke tells how he aspires to the crown and the means he intends to use to get it, and says:

> For this I have a largess from the Pope,
> A pension and a dispensation too;
> And by that privilege to work upon,
> My policy hath fram'd religion.
> Religion! *O Diabole!*
> Fie, I am ashamd, however that I seem,
> To think a word of such a simple sound,
> Of such great matter should be made the ground.

In addition to such direct references as these, it should be noted that the general tone of Marlowe's plays and the conception of his characters, their subordination of religion and everything else to their desires, are strongly reminiscent of Machiavelli. Edward Meyer is probably right when he says of Marlowe, "He had studied Machiavelli with a vengeance: and it may be stated as an absolute certainty, that had the 'Principe' never been written, his three great heroes would not have been drawn with such gigantic strokes."[21]

But there is a good deal of matter in the charges made against Marlowe that seems to have had no connection with Machiavellianism. The following passages from the Baines report, for instance, are of an entirely different tenor:

> He affirmeth that Moyses was but a Jugler, & that one Heriot being Sir W Raleighs man Can do more than he.
>
> That Moyses made the Jewes to travell XL yeares in the wildernes, (wch Journey might haue bin done in lesse then one yeare) ere they Came to the

---

[20] Alexander Dyce, *The Works of Marlowe*, I, 235.

[21] *Machiavelli and the Elizabethan Drama* (Weimar, 1897), pp. 33–34.

promised land, to thintent that those who were privy to most of his subtilties might perish and so an everlasting superstition Remain in the harts of the people. . . . .

That it was an easy matter for Moyses being brought vp in all the arts of the Egiptians to abuse the Jewes being a rude & grosse people.

That Christ was a bastard and his mother dishonest.

That he was the sonne of a Carpenter, and that if Jewes among whome he was borne did Crucify him theie best knew him and whence he came.

That Crist deserved better to dy then Barrabas and that the Jewes made a good Choise. though Barrabas were both a theif and a murtherer.

That the woman of Samaria & her sister were whores & that Christ knew them dishonestly.

That St. John the Evangelist was bedfellow to Christ and leaned alwaies in his bosome, that he vsed him as the sinners of Sodoma.[22]

This information is partly borne out by Kyd's letter to the Council from prison, in which Kyd says concerning Marlowe:

First it was his custom when I knewe him first and as I heare saie he con-
tynewed it in table talk or otherwise to jest at the devine scriptures gybe at
pariers, and stryve in arguint to frustrate and confute what hath byn spoke
or wrytt by prophets and such holie men.

1. He wold report St. John to be or savior Christes Alexis I cover it wt
reverence and trembling that is that Christ did loue him with an extraordinary
loue.

2. That for me to wryte a poem of St. paules conversion as I was determined he said wold be as if I shold go wryte a book of fast and loose, esteeming
Paul a Jugler.

3. That the prodigall Childs portion was but fower nobles, he held his
purse so neere the bottom in all the pictures. . . . .

4. That things esteemed to be donn by devine power might haue as well
been don by observation of men.[23]

These utterances are no doubt typical of the blasphemous scoffings so often attributed to atheists during the period, and there is here, it must be admitted, at least a suggestion of the famous book *De tribus impostoribus*. A tradition had been current ever since the thirteenth century that there was a book of that title proving Moses, Christ, and Mohammed to have been imposters, but whether any such work was actually written before the eighteenth century, when several of that title appeared, is much in doubt. Grosart is clearly going beyond the facts when he says:

[22] Tannenbaum, *The Booke of Sir Thomas Moore*, Appen. CC.
[23] Greg, *loc. cit.*

The principal source of these doctrines was the celebrated work "De tribus impostoribus mundi" which first appeared in the latter half of the sixteenth century, and was well known in England. . . . . There is not the slightest doubt that Marlowe was well acquainted with "De tribus impostoribus."[24]

There are nevertheless two points that deserve notice. In 1706 there came to light a Latin treatise in manuscript called *De tribus famosissimis deceptoribus* and addressed to *Otho illustrissimus*, conceivably Duke Otho of Bavaria (thirteenth century), and this was described but never printed.[25] There is still extant, at Paris, Dresden, and Munich, a work bearing the title *De tribus impostoribus, 1598*, and this was formerly thought to have been published at Vienna with the false date in 1753. But Wolfgang Kraemer has studied the work carefully and has reached the conclusion that it was really written during the sixteenth century.[26] Certainly, then, we cannot definitely say that no such work circulated in manuscript and that Marlowe did not read it. Even if we could be sure that Marlowe had never seen the book, we yet know that he had heard of it, and with nothing but the title to go on, a person of his fertility of imagination could readily have conjectured the information that such a book ought to contain.

The three deceivers of the world according to this work had been Moses, Christ, and Mohammed, but it would have been only natural for Kyd and Baines to have reported only what Marlowe had to say about the first two, since the Christian religion of course required a man to believe that Mohammed was an impostor. But Marlowe did not allow Mohammed to escape. Tamburlaine, in the second part of the play that bears his name, is made to burn the *Alcoran* and to mock its author in the following terms:

> Now, Mahomet, if thou have any power,
> Come down thyself and work a miracle:
> Thou are not worthy to be worshipped

[24] *Life and Works of Greene*, I, 35–36.

[25] J. M. Robertson, *History of Freethought*, I, 324.

[26] "Ein seltener Druck des Traktats 'De tribus Impostoribus, 1598,' " *Zeitschrift für Bücherfreunde*, N.F., XIV (1922), 101–11.

That suffer's flames of fire to burn the writ
Wherein the sum of thy religion rests. . . . .
Well, soldiers, Mahomet remains in hell;
He cannot hear the voice of Tamburlaine:
Seek out another godhead to adore;
The God that sits in heaven, if any god,
For he is God alone, and none but he.

We may now turn to another point that deserves passing mention. Kyd, it will be recalled, affirmed that the heretical fragment found among his papers was Marlowe's, but even if this were true I do not think we should conclude that Unitarianism played any great part in forming Marlowe's atheism. The fact of significance is that someone had enough interest in attacks on the divinity of Christ to copy the passages from Proctor's *Fal of the Late Arrian* supporting the thesis that Christ was only human, and to omit Proctor's refutations. In view of what we learn from other sources, it seems likely that Marlowe was curious about any kind of irreligious thought, and if he really owned this document, the fact is to be taken rather as indicative of his state of mind than responsible for it.

Some light may possibly be thrown on Marlowe's attitude toward religion by observing a little more in detail the company with which he consorted. For a time at least he was a member of the notable group of spies that Sir Francis Walsingham had assembled for the purpose of discovering and stamping out Catholic plots. Among this group he was undoubtedly associated with some of the most seditious and unprincipled men that the times could produce, for Walsingham, a believer in the old maxim "Set a thief to catch a thief," seems actually to have preferred men of known looseness of character. No doubt Sir Edward Stafford, the English ambassador at Paris, expressed Walsingham's as well as his own attitude when he wrote to Walsingham concerning the Catholic refugees at Paris in 1583, "I mean to use them all well if they come to me . . . . for my own part I am of a mind to use the devil himself well if he come to me in the likeness of a man to serve the queen withal."[27] It was Staf-

---

[27] Read, *op. cit.*, II, 410.

ford also who in 1588 in another letter to Walsingham revealed
the presence of an English atheist, one Roger Walton, at Paris,
apparently not knowing that he was one of Walsingham's spies:
"To some he showeth himself a great papist, to others a protestant, but as they take him who haunteth him most, he hath
neither God nor religion, a very evil condition, a swearer without measure and tearer of God, a notable whoremaster."[28]

In the Baines report it had been said of Marlowe that "into
every Company he Cometh he perswades men to *Atheism* willing them not to be afeard of bugbeares and hobgoblins," and
that "one Ric Cholmeley hath Confessed that he was perswaded
by Marloes Reasons to become an *Atheist*." Whether persuaded
by Marlowe or not, this Cholmeley appears to have been atheistical enough, as well as mutinous and seditious. Concerning
his activities another government spy turned in to Justice
Young an unsigned letter of a sufficiently damning nature:

> Right worshipfull, whereas I promised to sende you worde when Cholmeley
> was with me, these are to lett you understand that hee hath not yet been with
> mee, for he doth partely suspect that I will bewray his villanye and his
> companye. But yesterday hee sente two of his companions to mee to knowe
> if I woulde ioyne with him in familiarity, and bee one of their damnable crue.
> I sothed the villaynes with faire wordes in their follies because I wold thereby
> dive into the secrets of their develish hartes, that I mighte better bewray
> their purposes to draw her Maiestie's subiectes to bee Athiestes. Their prac-
> tise is after her Maiestie's decease to make a Kinge amonge themselues and
> live accordinge to their owne lawes, and this saieth Cholmeley willbee done
> easely, because they bee and shortely wilbe by his and his felowes persuasions
> as many of their opynions as of any other religion. Mr. Cholmeley, his man-
> ner of proceedinge in seducinge the queenes subiectes is firste to make slander-
> ous reportes of most noble peeres and honourable Counsilors, as the Lord
> Threasorer, the Lord Chamberlayn, the Lord Admirall, Sir Robert Cecill.
> These saithe hee, have profounde wittes, be sound Athiestes, and their lives
> and deeds showe that they thinke their soules doe ende, vanishe, and perishe
> with their bodies.[29]

We of course cannot be sure that Marlowe was actually a
member of this "damnable crue," but he does seem to have been
of much the same temper as these men, even to the point of

[28] *Ibid.*, quoting Harleian MSS 288, fol. 218.

[29] Quoted by F. S. Boas in *Fortnightly Review*, February, 1899.

sedition. According to Baines, he had said that "he had as good right to Coine as the queen of England," and in Kyd's second letter it was reported that "he wold pswade wth men of quallitie to goe vnto the K of Scotts whether I heare Royden is gon and where if he had liued he told me when I sawe him last he meant to be." From seeing the worst sides of both religions and from observing the machinations of those in authority, these spies had become utterly cynical and probably even atheistical, and there is every reason to think that Marlowe shared their opinions.

Now there is unfortunately very little more information at present available that can be brought to bear on the subject. It is perhaps worth noting of course that in *Doctor Faustus* Faustus at the beginning of the play is made to say:

> Philosophy is odious and obscure;
> Both law and physic are for petty wits;
> Divinity is basest of the three,
> Unpleasant, harsh, contemptible, and vild!

and somewhat later, while working a charm:

> Within this circle is Jehovah's name
> Forward and backward anagrammatis'd,

thus reminding us of Parson's charge that Raleigh in his school for atheists taught the scholars to spell God backward. In the course of an interview with Mephistopheles, Faustus also says, "Come, I think hell's a fable," but it would probably be a mistake to attach much importance to utterances so essentially a part of the business of the play as these are.

I am myself certainly not of a mind to reach any spectacular conclusions about Marlowe's religious unbelief, but it seems to me that Tucker Brooke is pushing conservatism too far when he says of Marlowe, "He seems not to have been believed, unless by the 'ignorant,' to be an atheist."[30] I suppose Professor Brooke would class Greene and Kyd with the "ignorant," for both of these rather well-known literary men, one of them a Master of Arts of Clare Hall at Cambridge, were clearly of the

[30] *Works and Life of Christopher Marlowe* (London, 1930), I, 37.

opinion that their great contemporary was an atheist, Greene even reporting that he had said, "There is no God." The word "atheism" in the sixteenth century, as everyone knows, was applied indiscriminately to almost any kind of irregularity in religion, to Unitarianism, to Anabaptism, to Machiavellianism, and sometimes even to mere wickedness. As the sixteenth century used the word, Marlowe was undoubtedly an atheist. With the exception of Greene's statement, which I think should not be allowed much weight, there is little more to indicate that he was one in the modern sense of the word, but if we are to accept as true any part of the charges of Baines and Kyd, we have no choice but to conclude that he did not believe in the divinity of Jesus Christ.

XI

The Atheism of Sir Walter Raleigh

THE so-called atheism of Sir Walter Raleigh was of a
very different kind from that of Marlowe, although
their names have been associated so long in discussions
of the subject that one might be pardoned for supposing that
they had common beliefs. The first charge of atheism against
Raleigh that has survived was that of the Jesuit Robert Parsons, who said in his *Responsio ad Elizabethae edictum*, published at Rome in 1592:

> Of Sir Walter Rawley's schoole of Atheism by the waye, and of the Con-
> jurer that is Master thereof, and of the diligence vsed to get yong gentlemen
> of this schoole, where in both Moyses, and our Sauior, the olde, and the new
> Testamente are iested at, and the schollers taughte amonge other thinges,
> to spell God backwards.[1]

Before too much weight is given to these charges, however, it
should be remembered that this Parsons was a notorious plotter
who had barely escaped from England with his life on account
of his complicity in the famous Babington plot. Like all spies,
he gained his information through devious and often corrupted
channels, and moreover there is little reason to believe, con-
sidering the nature and condition of the man, that he would
have scrupled to make the most of any evidence, no matter how
doubtful, that would represent his enemies in an unfavorable
light.

The next evidence that bears on the case is not directly
against Sir Walter himself but against one of his household, the
mathematician Harriot. Parsons mentioned a conjurer who was

---

[1] Quoted by Boas in *Marlowe and His Circle* (Oxford, 1929), pp. 70–71.

the master of the School of Atheism, no doubt referring to this man, and Baines in his report against Marlowe has Marlowe saying, "that Moyses was but a Jugler & that one Heriots being Sir W. Raleighs man can do more than he." Thomas Kyd in his letter to Puckering mentions Harriot, Warner, and Royden as associates of Marlowe and by implication partakers of his religious opinions, although Kyd hastens to add that he does not accuse them of atheism. Moreover, Baines reports of Marlowe that "he saith like wise that he hath quoted a number of Contrarities oute of Scripture which he hath given to some great men who in convenient time shalbe named." A convenient time may never have arrived for Baines, as he suffered the inconvenience of being hanged the following year, but it is an allowable conjecture, in view of subsequent developments, that one of these great men was Sir Walter himself.

But thus far Raleigh had not actually been named by any writer in England. It remained for an anonymous spy to perform that service. There is preserved in Harleian MSS 6848, folio 175, a note to the Privy Council, undated but probably written in the early summer of 1593, entitled "Remembrances of Wordes and Matter against Richard Cholmeley." In this, Cholmeley, also a spy, is accused of treachery, atheism, and murderous intentions, and is reported as saying that he "verely beleueth that one Marlowe is able to showe more sounde reasons for Atheisme than any devine in Englande is able to geue to prove devinitie, and that Marlowe tolde him that he hath read the Atheist lecture to Sir Walter Raleigh and others."

These are all the surviving documents in the case up to the middle of 1593. There had been only one direct charge, that of the Jesuit spy, safe in Rome, a man of unscrupulous character and with strong hatred for anyone connected with the English court. The spy Baines had mentioned Harriot and vaguely hinted at Sir Walter but had not accused them of anything. The anonymous spy reported Cholmeley as saying that Marlowe had said that he had read an atheistical lecture to Sir Walter, but accused Sir Walter of nothing. Kyd, not a spy, had under torture revealed the name of Harriot as an associate of Marlowe but disavowed any charge of atheism against him.

But however dubious the evidence may have been, the rumors and hearsay reports made a strong impression on the popular mind and were long remembered. And more important, apparently as a direct result of them, in March of 1594 a commission, "Her heighnes Comission for cawses Ecclesiasticall," was appointed to sit at Cerne Abbas, in Dorset, for the sole purpose of investigating atheism. The Commission met March 21, called witnesses, and put nine questions to them. Since these questions have only once before been printed in full in an English publication,[2] and since they form an important document in the history of sixteenth-century religious incredulity, I shall reproduce them here in full:

1. Inprimis whome doe you knowe, or have harde to be suspected of Atheisme; or Apostacye? And in what manner doe you knowe or have harde the same? And what other notice can you geive thereof?
2. Itm whome do you knowe, or have harde, that have argued, or spoken againste? or as doubtinge, the beinge of anye God? Or what or where God is? Or to sweare by god, addinge if there be a god, or such like, and when and where was the same? And what other notice can you geive of anye such offendr?
3. Itm whome doe you knowe or have harde that hath spoken againste god his providence ouer the worlde? or of the worldes beginninge or endinge? or of prdestinacion? or of heaven or of hell? or of the Resureccion in doubtfull or contenciouse manner? When and where was the same? And what other notice can you geive of anye such offendr?
4. Itm whome doe you knowe or have harde that hath spoken againste the truth of god his holye worde revealed to vs in the scriptures of the oulde & newe testament? or of some part thereof? or have sayde those scriptures ar not to be beleived & defended by her Majestie for doctrine, & faith, and salvacion, but onlie of policye, or Civell gouernment, and when and where was the same? And what other notice can you geive of anye such offendr?
5. Itm whome doe you knowe or have harde hath blasphemouslye cursed god: as sayinge one time (as it rayned when he was hawkinge) if there be a god A poxe on that god which sendeth such weather to marr our sporte? or such like. Or do you knowe or have harde of anye that hath broken froth into anye other wordes of blasphemye and when and where was the same.

---

[2] By G. B. Harrison in the Appendix to his edition of *Willobie His Avisa* (London, 1926). F. C. Danchin has also reprinted them in *Revue germanique*, November-December, 1913.

6. Itm whome doe you knowe or have harde to have sayde, when he was dead his soule shoulde be hanged on the topp of a poale, and ronne god, ronne devill, and fetch it that wolde have it, or to like effecte? or that hath otherwise spoken againste the beinge; or immortallitye of the soule of man? or that a mans soule shoulde dye and become like the soule of a beaste, or such like, and when and where was the same?

7. Itm whome doe you knowe or have harde hath Counselled, procured, ayded, Comforted, or conferred with anye such offendr? When where & in what manner was the same?

8. Itm whome doe you knowe or have harde of anye of those offendrs to affirme, all those that were not of there opinions towchinge the prmisses to be schismatickes, and in error. And whome doe you knowe hath so affirmed? And when and where was it spoken?

9. Itm what can you saye more of anye of the prmisses? or whome have you knowne or harde can geive anye notice of the same? And speak all your knowledge therein.[3]

The witnesses to whom these questions were put were nearly all village parsons of Dorsetshire, together with a few other villagers whom their testimonies made it necessary to summon. Nearly all the witnesses declared that they could give no definite information, that they knew nothing personally, but that they had heard Sir Walter Raleigh suspected of holding unorthodox religious opinions. A few mentioned Mr. Carew Raleigh and "one Herryott" of Sir Walter's house. The testimony of the curate of Motcombe is fairly typical:

John Davis Curate of Motcombe sworne & examined the daye and yeare above sayde. To the first Interogatory sayeth that he knoweth of noe such parson directlye, but he hath harde Sr Walter Rawleigh by generall reporte hath had some reasoninge against the dietye of god, and his omnipotencye. And hath harde the like of Mr. Carewe Rawleigh, but not soe directlye.

One parson recalled that "he harde Mr. Carewe Rawleigh saye at Gillingham there was a god in nature," and two or three others mentioned a Lieutenant Allen of Raleigh's house who was a light esteemer of religion and would not come to church.

To Mr. Fraunces Scarlett, minister of Sherborne, however, went the honor of furnishing the sensation of the day. This gentleman testified that as he walked down the streets of his native town, Robert Hyde, a shoemaker, called him into his shop. Hyde told Scarlett that he was sorry to say that after all the

---

[3] Harrison, *op. cit.*, pp. 255–57.

good preaching they had listened to in that town about heaven
and hell, there was nevertheless a company of people there who
said hell was only poverty and suffering and heaven only riches
and enjoyment, and there was no life after death. Hyde was
promptly called before the Commission and asked to give further information about the company he knew of. Then, however, he swore that

for his owne part he doth knowe noe such; neither can bringe anye aucthoure
for such reports. but the reasons which moved him to vse such speches was
some conference had with a brother of his, whoe dwellinge at Milborne porte
toulde this depont that he harde Mr. Davidge preache at Sturton Caundell
deliuer in the pulpitt that there was such a sectt which he did there seeme to
confute.[4]

Mr. Scarlett also made known that in his parish some time
back two matrons while walking home from church with a serv-
ing man named Olliver had taken occasion to praise the sermon
they had just heard. This Olliver then retorted that in the first
place the sermon could have been much shorter, and in the second a correct account had not been given of Moses, who, Olliver
avowed, in reality had had forty whores, of whom the preacher
had made no mention. The gentlewomen said that "there eares
did glowe, and that they neuer harde such mounsterous speches
from anye man," but when they were finally brought before the
Commission it turned out that Olliver, no great Bible scholar, it
seems, had merely confused Moses and Solomon, and moreover
that he had been drunk at the time he did it.

These absurdities serve at least to illustrate to what lengths
the clergy was willing to go to prove to the Commission that
there was atheism in England. But the real purpose of the inquiry, one suspects, was to fix a charge of atheism on Sir Walter,
and, if so, it had thus far failed. Nothing even resembling real

[4] To what extent the clergy themselves were responsible for the notion that atheism
was widespread in England is an interesting field for conjecture. Knocking down men
of straw is not always as innocuous a sport as it seems, since some may not recognize
that they are men of straw. Moreover, to others the victory may not seem very de-
cisive. Benjamin Franklin said in his *Autobiography* that he first became an unbeliever
from reading a preacher's refutation of atheism, wherein the arguments of the atheist
seemed to him stronger than those of the preacher.

evidence had been brought forward. In the latter course of the investigation, however, Ralph Ironside, minister of Winterbottom, was sworn and proceeded to give some first-hand evidence. Ironside had actually been present at one of the famous table conferences attended by Raleigh and others where atheism was popularly supposed to have been taught, and thus his evidence is of the first importance among so much rumor and hearsay. It is not likely that he varied very far from the truth in his account, for Sir Ralph Horsey, who had been with him at the meeting, was also on the very Commission before which he was testifying.

One night in the summer of 1593, said Ironside, he had gone with Sir Walter Raleigh, his brother Mr. Carew Raleigh, and Sir Ralph Horsey to supper at the table of Sir George Trenchard at Wolverton. After supper the conversation turned on the soul, and Mr. Carew Raleigh posed the question what the soul really was. To this Sir Walter replied:

> I have been (sayeth he) a scholler some tyme in Oxeforde, I have aunswered vnder Bachelor of Arte & had taulke with diuines, yet heithervnto in this pointe (to witt what the reasonable soule of man is) have I not by anye benne resolved. They tell vs it is *Primus motor* the first mover in a man etc.[5]

Ironside undertook to satisfy both of them by quoting the definition of the soul in Aristotle's *De anima*, but Sir Walter, in this respect at least no good "Clerk of Oxenford," repudiated the Aristotelian definition as too obscure and intricate to satisfy anyone. At a later stage of the discussion he also found fault with Aristotle's definition of God as "Ens Entium" for the same reason and said, "Neither coulde I lerne heitherto what god is."

Ironside remembered nothing else that should be mentioned to the Commission and with his testimony the Commission closed its inquiry. It had learned, what was already well known, that Sir Walter and various members of his house were popularly supposed to be incredulous about certain points of the Christian doctrine. More specifically it had found out that he discussed God and the soul philosophically rather than theo-

[5] Harrison, *op. cit.*, p. 262. Boas also reprints Ironside's testimony in his recent book, *op. cit.*

logically and that he did not accept Aristotle's definition of either. None of these things could be called atheism or even heresy, not even according to the strictest interpretations of the day. Sir Walter had in effect been given a clean bill of health, and during the next ten years very few if any imputations against his religious beliefs found their way into print.

After the death of Essex in 1601, for some reason never fully explained, Robert Cecil, formerly Raleigh's friend, turned against him and began to seek his ruin. Cecil was in secret correspondence with James for two years before his accession to the throne and had not only thoroughly ingratiated himself with that monarch but had predisposed him against Raleigh. With James and Cecil as well as other powerful enemies, notably Lord Thomas Howard, anxious to bring about his downfall, it may be supposed that if it had been possible to gain any real evidence of Raleigh's atheism it would have been brought forward at this time. But when the blow fell, in November, 1603, it was for complicity in a plot with Lord Cobham to put Arabella Stuart on the throne of England with the aid of Spain.

There are, however, incident to Raleigh's trial a number of references to his atheism that throw some further light on the matter. For instance, at one point in the trial the information came out that Raleigh had written to Lord Cobham not to take any preachers into his confidence and not to be overtaken by them as Essex was. On hearing this, the King's attorney, Edward Coke, who had prosecuted the charges with the greatest acrimony, cried out, "O! damnable atheist! He hath learnt some text of Scripture to serve his own purpose, but falsely alledged. He counsels him not to be counselled by preachers as Essex was. He died the child of God, God honoured him at his death."[6] Raleigh had not expressed any atheistical opinions and had quoted no Scripture, but Coke had heard of his atheism and thought this a good time to mention it, of course for the benefit of the jury.

---

[6] Arthur Cayley, *Life of Sir Walter Ralegh*, I, 428. Cayley prints the whole proceedings of the trial along with a number of letters that bear on it.

A less prejudiced witness and one likely to be better informed was Sir John Harrington. Harrington, like Ironside, had actually been present at one of the table conferences in Raleigh's house where religious matters were discussed. During the course of Raleigh's trial, in a letter to Dr. John Still, bishop of Bath and Wells, Harrington said:

I wist not that he [Raleigh] hath evil design in point of faith or religion. As he hath oft discoursed to me with much learning, wisdom, and freedom, I know he doth somewhat differ in opinion from some others, but I think also his heart is well fixed in every honest thing, a far as I can look into him. . . . . In religion, he hath shewn (in private talk) great depth and good reading, as I once experienced at his own house, before many learned men.[7]

Once again in the course of the trial the suspicion of atheism against Raleigh received mention, this time from the lord chief justice himself. Just before pronouncing the death penalty, Lord Chief Justice Popham thought it necessary to say:

You have been taxed by the world with the defense of the most heathenish and blasphemous opinions; which I list not to repeat, because christian ears cannot endure to hear them, nor the authors and maintainers of them be suffered to live in any christian commonwealth. You know what men said of Harpool. You shall do well before you go out of the world, to give satisfaction therein; and do not die with these imputations on you. Let not any devil persuade you to think there is no eternity in heaven. For if you think thus, you shall find eternity in hell-fire.[8]

Popham then condemned Raleigh in accordance with the regulation sentence for treason to a horrible and shameful death, but, as everyone knows, the sentence was not carried out. Instead he was confined in the Tower at the King's pleasure and languished there for over twelve years. Then came the disastrous voyage to Guiana, from which he returned to be executed for piracy in 1618, but at least dying the death of a gentleman beneath the ax. In that year Sir Thomas Lorkin wrote to Sir Thomas Puckering describing the execution, and we learn that the suspicion of atheism had pursued Sir Walter to the last:

[7] *Ibid.*, II, 456–57.

[8] *Ibid.*, I, 433. No attempt to identify Harpool has ever been successful. My own opinion is that the chief justice meant Marlowe.

Being come to the scaffold, he saw the lords seated in a place that was provided for them, somewhat far off, and fearing lest his voice should not well reach them, desired them that they would approach, because what he had then to say he wished the whole world should take notice of; and so they did, and heard a most grave, Christian, and elegant discourse, as they commonly qualify it. In it he laboured to clear himself from three main aspersions. The first, of atheism, which he did, by a worthy profession of his faith, and profession of his hope to be saved thereby.[9]

If from this mass of confusing and sometimes contradictory documents one turns to what Raleigh himself wrote in hopes of finding some clearer expression of religious incredulity, he is sure to be disappointed. He left behind him, to be sure, a considerable body of work, but most of it, aside from his *History of the World*, of a practical or occasional nature that precludes any religious or philosophical reflections. In such works as *A Discourse Touching the War with Spain*, *The Origin of War*, and *The Discovery of Guiana* there is naturally hardly a reference to religion, and little more in the *History of the World*, although it begins with some pious observations of a strictly conventional character.

In the more personal works, such as his letters and his *Instructions to His Son*, one finds likewise mostly practical considerations. The son is advised to use great care in choosing a wife, to avoid private quarrels, and not to seek riches by evil means. There is almost no religion in it until at the end when Sir Walter says:

Serve God, let him be the Author of all thy Actions, commend all thy Endeavours to him that must either wither or prosper them, please him with Prayer, lest if he frown he confound all thy Fortunes and Labours, like the Drops of Rain on the sandy Ground. Let my experienced Advice, and fatherly Instructions, sink deep into thy Heart. So God direct thee in all his Ways, and fill thy Heart with his Grace.[10]

The letter he wrote to his wife the night before he thought he was to be executed in 1603 is similar in tone to this:

God is my witness I meant you all my Office of Wines . . . . but God hath prevented all my resolutions, even that great God that ruleth all in all: But if you can live free from Want, care for no more, the rest is but Vanity; love

[9] *Ibid.*, II, 415.　　　[10] Thomas Birch, *The Works of Sir Walter Raleigh*, II, 357.

God, and begin betimes to repose yourself on him; and therein shall you find
true and lasting Riches, and endless Comfort. . . . . Teach your Son also to
love and fear God, whilst he is yet young, that the Fear of God may grow up
in him; and then God will be a Husband to you, and a Father to him. . . . .

The everlasting, powerful, infinite, and omnipotent God; who is Goodness
itself; the true Life and true Light keep thee and thine, have Mercy on me,
and teach me to forgive my Persecutors and Accusers, and send us to meet in
his glorious Kingdom.[11]

A discussion of Raleigh's poetry is always rendered difficult
by the fact that it is well-nigh impossible to determine what he
wrote. He is known to have written the two sonnets at the beginning of Spenser's *Faerie Queene*, and two or three others are
ascribed to him with some reason, but the rest are doubtful.
But if he wrote the entire twenty-nine included in Egerton
Brydges' collection[12] it would still be impossible to determine
anything from them about his religious beliefs. Most of them
are love poems and light lyrics. Of the rest, there is a dialogue
between God and the soul, deeply religious in tone, a poem on
death in which the five ages of man are reviewed, and, best
known of all, the extraordinary poem "His Pilgrimage." This
last, which I regard as pretty certainly Raleigh's, is a queer mixture of sentiment and realism and at least shows an unconven-
tional attitude toward life after death. Other than that little
can be deduced from it, however, and it as well as the rest of
the poems shows no evidence of religious incredulity.

If anywhere in his writings Raleigh might be expected to give
expression to his philosophical opinions, it would be in his two
essays "The Sceptick" and the "Treatise of the Soul," both of
which have promising titles. The first of these we discover,
however, to be a summary of the first three tropes of the *Pyrrhonean Hypotyposes* of Sextus Empiricus. The following passages, selected from near the beginning of the first trope, will
show how closely Raleigh followed his model:[13]

[11] *Ibid.*, pp. 384–85.

[12] *The Poems of Sir Walter Raleigh* (2d ed.; London, 1814).

[13] Birch's edition of Raleigh's Works, II, 331 ff., and the translation of the *Pyrrhonean Sketches* by Mary Patrick, *Sextus Empiricus and Greek Skepticism* (Cambridge,
1899), pp. 113 ff.

SEXTUS

In regard to the differences in origin, some animals originate without mixture of the sexes, while other originate through sexual intercourse. Of those which originate without intercourse of the sexes, some come from fire, as the little animals which appear in the chimneys, others from stagnant water, as musquitoes, others from fermented wine, as the stinging ants, others from the earth, others from the mud, like the frogs, others from slime, as the worms, others from donkeys, as the beetles, others from cabbage, as caterpillars, others from fruit, as the gall insect from the wild figs, others from putrefied animals, as bees from bulls, and wasps from horses.

Again, of those originating of intercourse of the sexes, some come from animals of the same kind, as in most cases, and others from those of different kinds, as mules. Again of animals in general, some are born alive, as men, others from eggs, as birds, and others are born a lump of flesh, as bears. It is probable therefore, that the inequalities and differences in origin cause great antipathies in the animals, and the result is incompatibility, discord, and conflict between the sensations of different animals.

RALEIGH

Some living Creatures are by Copulation and some without it: and that either by Fire, as crickets in Furnaces; or corrupt Water, as Gnats; or Slime, as Frogs; or Dirt, as Worms; or Herbs, as Cankerworms; some from Ashes,[14] as Beetles; some from Trees, as the Worm Psenas bred in the wild Fig-tree; some of living Creatures putrified, as Bees of Bulls, and Wasps of Horses.

By Copulation many Creatures are brought forth alive as Man; some in the Egg, as Birds; some in an unshapen piece of Flesh, as Bears. These great Differences cannot but cause a divers and contrary Temperament, and Quality in those Creatures; and consequently, a great Diversity in their Fancy and Conceit.

Sextus, of course, following his master Pyrrho, proceeds to argue that because of the differences in sensory perceptions among men and animals, we are unable to be sure that we alone perceive truly, and that consequently all is in doubt, not only our conceptions of material things but our philosophical opinions as well. Most of Raleigh's fragment, only eight pages in length, deals with the physical and psychological bases of skepti-

[14] Raleigh no doubt wrote "Asses."

cism, but toward the end he includes a passage in which the
philosophical aspects of the system are somewhat touched upon:

> To believe what all Man say of one and the same thing is not possible; for
> then we shall believe Contrarieties; for some Men say, that that very Thing is
> pleasant, which others say is displeasant. If it be said we must believe only
> some Men, then let it be shewed who these men are; for the Platonists will
> believe Plato, but the Epicures Epicurus, the Pythagoreans Pythagoras, and
> other Philosophers the Masters of their own Sects: so it is doubtful, to which
> of all these we shall give credit. If it be said we must credit the greatest Num-
> ber; this seemeth childish; for there be amongst other nations a greater Num-
> ber which deny that very Point, which the greatest Number with us do affirm;
> so that hereof nothing can certainly be affirmed.[15]

Now this summary or free translation of the Pyrrhonic doctrine would seem to indicate an interest in philosophy on
Raleigh's part, but unfortunately for our purpose we are not
able to draw any very far-reaching conclusions from it in regard
to Raleigh's so-called atheism. It is true that in some respects
Pyrrhonism made for religious doubt and unbelief, for an active
mind would go on from sensory impressions and philosophies to
doubt religious revelations as well. By encouraging a comparison of all religions Pyrrhonism cleared the way for deism, and it
was the current of thought most responsible for the attitude toward religion that we find in Montaigne. On the other hand, as
we have seen, the system of Pyrrho and Sextus was taken over,
with some modifications, by the Christian apologists themselves
quite early in the Renaissance and made the basis for attacks
on human learning, the Christian religion alone being excepted
from the Pyrrhonic conclusions.

There is nothing connected with Raleigh's free translation itself to show with which of these developments he was most in
line. With nothing but the fragment to go on, we can only say
that it may have been either or that his interest in the subject
may have been purely academic. It should be observed that
Henri Etienne translated all of Sextus from Greek into Latin
between 1562 and 1569, but was so far from being influenced
toward unbelief by his work that in his *Apologie pour Hèrodote*

---

[15] Birch, *op. cit.*, II, 338-39.

(Geneva, 1566) he indignantly denounced the atheists of his time. Nevertheless, it is entirely possible that Pyrrhonism encouraged in Raleigh a critical attitude toward religion, a disposition to speculate about it and to consider it philosophically, that would have been strongly deprecated by the clergy and that would have offered an advantageous point of attack for his enemies.

The *Treatise of the Soul* is a well-planned tract, twenty pages in length, which handles its subject in a formal and thoroughly conventional fashion. The date of its composition is not known, but it was probably written after 1603, like most of Raleigh's works, and it is clear that it was written under the influence of such works as Woolton's *Treatise of the Immortalitie of the Soule*, Mornay's *Trunesse of the Christian Religion*, and Davies' *Nosce Teipsum*. Sir Walter begins by gravely laying down the Aristotelian precept that there are three souls in man, the vegetative, the sensitive or animal, and the reasonable soul, this last soul the one that distinguishes man from the brute creation. Concerning the nature of this reasonable soul he adds:

> The substance of the soul is hardly known; Lactantius denieth that men can attain to the knowledge of the nature of the soul; and Galen confesseth, that he cannot tell what or where the substance of the soul is. And Athanasius saith that while we live there are three things whereof we cannot attain the knowledge; the substance of God, of angels, and of our souls.[16]

Raleigh then reviews the various theories about how individual souls are created, refutes unorthodox opinions on the subject, and himself takes the position, in line with the best theological thought of the day, that God creates a soul for each man as he is born. Next comes a psychological discussion, quite similar to those of Primaudaye and Davies on the same subject, of the powers of the soul. The soul, it appears, has two senses, the inward and the outer. The outer consists of the five bodily

[16] *Ibid.*, VIII, 574. Ironside's testimony before the Commission at Cerne Abbas will need to be recalled at this point. Ironside thought the fact that Raleigh had denied any knowledge of the nature of the soul or of God to be of sufficient importance to mention to the Commission, but here we find that he does not scruple to say the same thing openly and to call the Church Fathers to his support.

senses, the inward of the mental faculties, common sense, judgment, imagination, and memory.

Finally, the soul is declared immortal and the testimonies and evidence are adduced, not exhaustively, as with Woolton and Mornay, but sufficiently to show that he is writing in their tradition:

> The soul of man, using will and reason, is immortal. Galen reporteth that all wise men unto Plato were of that opinion; but some latter persons, being overcome by their own folly, constrained not only their bodies but their souls also, as it were to die. . . . . Last of all; religion, and the fear of God, which is in man doth shew it to be immortal, for we worship God because our souls are made in his image, and we know he is *a rewarder of them* that serve him.[17]

Thus the investigation of the charge that Raleigh kept a school for atheism where the Old and New Testaments were jested at, far from substantiating the charge, has actually led us to range Sir Walter with the Christian apologists, with Woolton, Sir John Davies, and Henry Smith in England, with Charles de Bourgueville and Philip Mornay in France, the men who were trying to stem the currents of unbelief flowing into France and England from Italy. Of course it may be urged that Sir Walter wrote his *Treatise of the Soul* as a deliberate attempt to establish his orthodoxy and lay the frequently voiced suspicions, that the *Treatise* does not represent his real opinion. Such a conjecture, however, is without any documentary support, and a strong argument against it is the complete breakdown of the Cerne Abbas Commission and its failure to bring to light any evidence worthy the name. A still stronger argument, it seems to me, is the fact that two men who were actually with Sir Walter at the table when philosophy and religion were being discussed, Ralph Ironside and Sir John Harrington, give reports of his opinions that coincide perfectly with the view set forth in the *Treatise of the Soul*. If then this *Treatise* really represents Raleigh's mature religious beliefs, and it seems to me that there ought not to be much doubt that it does, his opinions are no

[17] *Ibid.*, pp. 589, 591.

more to be objected to than those of Bishop Woolton and Sir John Davies.

Is there any reason to believe that Raleigh was inclined toward atheism in his youth, or that he encouraged unbelief among the members of his household? That is a field for speculation. But if one wishes to speculate, a fact worth remembering is that Raleigh spent six years of his youth in France,[18] 1569–75, where atheism, according to contemporary writers, was exceedingly prevalent. We have already touched on this matter in the previous chapters and have observed how the various currents of free thought had gained strong headway in France thirty or forty years before they reached important proportions in England. We have observed especially how from about 1525 on the tenets of the Paduan school about the eternity of the world, the providence of God, the credibility of miracles, and the immortality of the soul began to be known and discussed in France. The teaching of Francisco Vicomercato and other disciples of Pomponazzi in France lent great impetus to these discussions, and from 1550 on it seems to have become a fad in court circles to debate the Paduan tenets, if not actually to believe them, much to the consternation of the clergy and all true Christians, as their numerous books against atheism eloquently testify.

It is unlikely that a young Englishman should in the midst of this period spend six years in the courts of France without hearing many of these debates and without becoming familiar with the general course of the speculations. Raleigh was at the impressionable age when a man's philosophy and religious ideas usually begin to take some definite form, and he may have admired the boldness of speculation and the free play of intellect that he witnessed in France. It may be moreover that upon returning to England and receiving advancement at court he harbored the idea of surrounding himself with a number of free spirits who would welcome philosophical discussions, perhaps

[18] Cayley, *op. cit.*, I, 11–14.

partly because of his own interest and partly because he wished to be recognized as a patron of scholars and advanced thinkers.[19]

If such a group were formed, it is more than likely that the Pomponazzian questions would sooner or later be touched upon, but there is no evidence to show that Raleigh or any of his group ever followed them very far or that they reached Pomponazzi's conclusions.[20] The evidence in truth points in the other direction. The nature of the soul and its faculties, the evidences of its immortality, the nature of God, the function of religion in a state and similar questions may have been discussed with some freedom, as they were constantly being discussed by men of unimpeachable orthodoxy. But whatever the nature of the discussions, they were not long continued. For whether from lack of further inclination, or from press of practical affairs, or from fear of consequences in an England most inhospitable to any kind of religious irregularity, Raleigh soon threw his energies in other directions. He may in his youth have passed through a period of doubt, but age at any rate found him orthodox and even one of the defenders of Christian dogma.

[19] His patronage of Spenser may have been part of such a program.

[20] It should nevertheless be observed that the Cerne Abbas Commission certainly expected something of the kind. Questions 3 and 6, with the exception of a definite rumor they had heard of blasphemy, verge very closely on the main problems posed by Pomponazzi.

SELECTED BIBLIOGRAPHY

ORIGINAL SOURCES

AGRIPPA, HENRY CORNELIUS. *The Vanity of Arts and Sciences*. London, 1684.

ANVERS, HENRY D'. *A Treatise of Baptism*. London, 1674.

ARISTOTLE. *De anima*. Translated by R. D. HICKS. Cambridge University Press, 1907.

AUGUSTINE. *Confessions of Augustine*. Edited by W. G. T. SHEDD. Boston, 1867.

Augustini, Sancti Aurelii, Operum. Bassani, MDCCCVII.

BABINGTON, GERVASE. *The Workes of the Right Reverend Father in God Gervase Babington*, London, 1622.

BARTAS, GUILLAUME DU. *The Divine Weeks*. Translated by JOSHUA SYLVESTER and edited by GROSART in the *Complete Works of Joshua Sylvester*. 2 vols. London, 1877.

BACON, FRANCIS. *The Moral and Historical Works of Lord Bacon*. Edited by JOSEPH DEVEY. London, 1868.

——. *The Works of Francis Bacon*. Edited by SPEDDING, ELLIS, and HEATH. London, 1859.

BEARD, THOMAS. *The Theatre of Gods Ivdgements*. London, 1631.

BILSON, THOMAS. *The True Difference betweene Christian Subjection and Unchristian Rebellion*. Oxford, 1585.

BODIN, JEAN. *Colloque de Jean Bodin des secrets caches des choses sublimes entre sept scavans qui sont de differens sentemens*. Traduction française de ROGER CHAUVIRÉ. Paris, 1914.

BULLINGER, HENRY. *Adversus Anabaptistas Libri VI*. Zurich, M.D.LX.

——. *The Decades of Henry Bullinger*. Parker Society ed. Cambridge University Press, 1851.

CALVIN, JOHN. *The Institutes of the Christian Religion*. Translated by HENRY BEVERIDGE. 2 vols. Edinburgh, 1895.

CHEYNELL, FREDERICK. *The Rise, Growth, and Danger of Socinianisme*. London, 1643.

CICERO. *De natura deorum libri tres*. Edited by AUSTIN STICKNER. Boston, 1881.

——. *Of the Nature of the Gods and Divinations*. Edited by C. D. YOUNGE. London, 1907.

CRANMER, THOMAS. *The Remains of Thomas Cranmer*. Edited by HENRY JENKYNS. 4 vols. Oxford University Press, 1833.

DAVIES, JOHN, OF HEREFORD. *The Complete Works of John Davies of Hereford*. Edited by A. B. GROSART. 2 vols. London, 1878.

DAVIES, SIR JOHN. *The Complete Poems of Sir John Davies*. Edited by A. B. GROSART. 2 vols. London, 1876.

DOVE, JOHN. *Confutation of Atheism.* London, 1605.

ELYOT, SIR THOMAS. *The Boke Named the Gouernour.* Edited by H. S. CROFT. London, 1883.

FEATLEY, DANIEL. *The Dippers Dipt, or the Anabaptists Duck'd and Plung'd Head and Ears.* London, 1647.

GENTILLET, INNOCENT. *A Discovrs vpon the meanes of Wel Governing and Maintaining in good Peace; a Kingdom, or other Principalitie.* London, 1608.

GREENE, ROBERT. *The Life and Complete Works of Robert Greene.* Edited by A. B. GROSART. 15 vols. London, 1881–83.

GREG, W. W. (ed.). *Literary Autographs from 1550 to 1650.* Oxford University Press, 1925.

GREVILLE, FULKE, LORD BROOKE. *The Complete Works of Fulke Greville, Lord Brooke.* Edited by A. B. GROSART. 4 vols. London, 1870.

GRIFFITHS, JOHN (ed.). *The Two Books of Homilies Appointed To Be Read in Churches.* Oxford University Press, 1859.

HARRISON, G. B. (ed.). *Willobie His Avisa (1594).* London, 1926.

HARVEY, GABRIEL. *The Complete Works of Gabriel Harvey.* Edited by A. B. GROSART. London, 1884–85.

———. *Marginalia.* Edited by G. C. MOORE SMITH. Stratford-upon-Avon, 1913.

HERBERT, EDWARD. *Autobiography of Edward, Lord Herbert of Cherbury.* Edited by W. H. DIRCKS. London, 1888.

HERMINJARD, A. L. (ed.). *Correspondance des réformateurs.* 9 vols. Geneva, 1878–79.

HUTCHINSON, ROGER. *The Works of Roger Hutchinson.* Parker Society reprint, 1842.

KNEWSTUBS, J. *A Confutation of Certain Monstrous Heresies Taught by H. N.* London, 1579.

LACTANTIUS. *The Works of Lactantius.* Translated by WILLIAM FLETCHER. Edinburgh, 1871.

LATIMER, HUGH. *Seven Sermons before Edward VI (1549).* Arber reprint.

LODGE, THOMAS. *Wits Miserie and the Worlds Madnesse.* Edited by GOSSE. London, 1879.

LUCIAN. *The Works of Lucian of Samosata.* Translated by H. W. and F. S. FOWLER. Clarendon Press, 1905.

LUCRETIUS. *T. Lucreti Cari De rerum natura libri sex.* Edited by H. A. J. MUNRO. London, 1900.

———. *His Six Books of Epicurean Philosophy.* Translated by THOMAS CREECH. London, 1683.

LYLY, JOHN. *Euphues.* Edited by CROLL and CLEMON. London, 1916.

MACHIAVELLI, NICCOLO. *The Works of Nicholas Machiavelli.* Edited by H. NEVILE. London, 1675.

MARLOWE, CHRISTOPHER. *Selected Plays.* Edited by HAVELOCK ELLIS for the "Mermaid Series."

MIDDLETON, THOMAS. *The Works of Thomas Middleton.* Edited by A. H. BULLEN. London, 1885.

MONTAIGNE, MICHAEL, LORD OF. *Essayes*. Translated by JOHN FLORIO in 1603. 3 vols. Everyman edition.

MORE, SIR THOMAS. *Utopia*. Edited by GEORGE SAMPSON. London, 1914.

MORNAY, PHILIP. *The Knowledge of a Mans Owne Selfe*. London, 1602.

————. *A Worke Concerning the Trunesse of the Christian Religion: Against Atheists, Epicures, Paynims, Jews, Mahumetists, and Other Infidels*. London, 1617.

NASHE, THOMAS. *Pierce Penilesse His Supplication to the Divell*. Edited by G. B. HARRISON. London, 1924.

————. *The Works of Thomas Nashe*. Edited by R. B. MCKERROW. 5 vols. London, 1910.

NEMESIUS. *The Nature of Man*. Translated by GEORGE WITHER. London, 1636.

NOUE, FRANÇOIS DE LA. *The Politike and Militarie Discourses*. Translated by E. AGGAS. London, 1588.

PLATO. *The Republic*. Translated by H. SPENS. London, 1929.

PLINY, C. SECUNDUS. *The Historie of the World*. Translated by PHILEMON HOLLAND. London, 1634.

PLUTARCH. *Plutarch's Morals*. Edited by C. W. KING. London, 1889.

POMPONAZZI, PIETRO. *De immortalitate animae*. Venetijs, MDXXV.

PRIMAUDAYE, PIERRE DE LA. *The French Academie*. Translated by T[HOMAS] B[OWES]. London, 1618.

PROCTOR, JOHN. *The Fal of the Late Arrian*. London, 1549.

RALEIGH, SIR WALTER. *The Works of Sir Walter Raleigh*. Edited by THOMAS BIRCH. 2 vols. London, 1751.

————. *The Works of Sir Walter Raleigh*. 8 vols. Oxford University Press, 1829.

RASTELL, JOHN. *A New Boke of Purgatory, Whiche Is a Dyaloge betwene Comyngo & Gyngemyn*. London, 1530(?).

ROGERS, THOMAS. *An Exposition of the Thirty-nine Articles (1586)*. Parker Society reprint, 1854.

SIDNEY, SIR PHILIP. *The Arcadia*. Edited by H. O. SOMERS. London, 1891.

————. *The Defense of Poesie*. Edited by ALBERT FEUILLERAT. Cambridge, 1923.

SMITH, GREGORY (ed.). *Elizabethan Critical Essays*. 2 vols. Clarendon Press, 1904.

SMITH, HENRY. *The Works of Henry Smith*. Edinburgh, 1867.

STUBBS, PHILIP. *Anatomy of Abuses*. Edited by FURNIVALL for the New Shakespeare Society, 1877-79.

UDALL, JOHN. *A Demonstration of Discipline*. Edited by ARBER for the Scholar's Library. London, 1880.

VIRET, PIERRE. *The Worlde Possessed with Deuils*. Translated by T. S. London, 1583.

VIVES, LODOVICI. *De veritate fidei Christianae . . . . contra Ethnicos, Iudaeos, Agarenos, sive Mahumetanos, et peruerse Christianos*. Basileae, MDXLIV.

WILKINSON, WILLIAM. *A Confutation of Certain Articles Deliuered by H. N. vnto the Familie of Loue*. London, 1579.

WOOLTON, JOHN. *A Treatise of the Immortalitie of the Soule*. London, 1576.

STUDIES AND ARTICLES

ALLEN, J. H. *The Unitarian Movement since the Reformation*. New York, 1894.

ALLEN, J. W. *A History of Political Thought in the Sixteenth Century*. New York, 1928.

ARNOLD, E. VERNON. *Roman Stoicism*. Cambridge University Press, 1911.

ASHTON, H. *Du Bartas en Angleterre*. Paris, 1908.

BAX, E. B. *Rise and Fall of the Anabaptists*. London, 1903.

BAYLE, PIERRE. *Dictionaire historique et critique*. Rotterdam, 1720.

BERDAN, J. M. *Early Tudor Poetry*. New York, 1920.

BEZOLD, F. "Jean Bodins Colloquium Heptaplomeres und der Atheismus des 16. Jahrhunderts," *Historische Zeitschrift*, CXIII (1914), 260–315. Zweiter Teil, CXIV (1915), 237–301.

BOAS, F. S. *Marlowe and His Circle*. Oxford University Press, 1929.

———. "New Light on Marlowe and Kyd," *Fortnightly Review*, February, 1899, pp. 212–25.

BONET-MAURY, GASTON. *Des origines du christianisme unitaire chez les Anglais*. Paris, 1881.

BREDVOLD, LOUIS I. "Deism before Donne," *Papers of the Michigan Academy of Arts and Sciences*, IV (1924), 431 ff.

———. "The Sources Used by Sir John Davies for 'Nosce Teipsum,'" *Publications of the Modern Language Association*, XXXVIII (1923), 745–69.

BRIE, FRIEDRICH. "Deismus und Atheismus in der englischen Renaissance," *Anglia*, XLVIII (1928), 54–98, 105–68.

BRIGGS, W. D. "On a Document concerning Christopher Marlowe," *Studies in Philology*, XX (1923), 153–59.

BROOKE, C. F. TUCKER. *The Life of Marlowe and the Tragedy of Dido Queen of Carthage*. New York, 1930.

BUSSON, HENRI. *Les sources et le développement du rationalisme dans la littérature française de la renaissance (1533–1601)*. Paris, 1922.

CATROU, FRANÇOIS. *Histoire des Anabaptistes*. Amsterdam, 1699.

CAYLEY, ARTHUR. *Life of Sir Walter Ralegh*. 2 vols. London, 1806.

CHARBONNEL, J. *La pensée italienne au XVIe siècle*. Paris, 1919.

CHOLLET, L'ABBÉ. *La morale stoïcienne en face de la morale chrétienne*. Paris, 1898.

CHRISTIE, R. C. *Étienne Dolet, the Martyr of the Renaissance*. London, 1880.

CUNLIFFE, JOHN W. *The Influence of Seneca on Elizabethan Tragedy*. London, 1893.

DOUGLAS, A. H. *Pietro Pomponazzi*. Cambridge University Press, 1910.

⸸ EDWARDS, JOHN. *The Socinian Creed, Wherein Is Shew'd the Tendency to Irreligion and Atheism*. London, 1697.

GILSON, ÉTIENNE. *Saint Thomas d'Aquin*. Paris, 1925.

⸸ GRAY, AUSTIN K. "Some Observations on Christopher Marlowe, Government Agent," *Publications of the Modern Language Association*, XLIII (1928), 682–700.

GREENLAW, EDWIN. "The Captivity Episode in Sidney's 'Arcadia,'" *Manly Anniversary Studies* (Chicago, 1923), pp. 54–63.

HAILE, MARTIN. *Life of Reginald Pole.* New York, 1910.

HASTINGS, JAMES. *Encyclopedia of Religion and Ethics.* New York, 1908.

HEIDRICH, HANS. *John Davies of Hereford und sein Bild von Shakespeares Umgebung.* Leipzig, 1925.

HOGREFE, PEARL. "Elyot and 'The Boke Called Cortigiano in Ytalione,'" *Modern Philology,* XXVII (1930), 303–9.

HORROCKS, J. W. *Machiavelli in Tudor Opinion and Discussion.* New York, 1908.

HOTSON, J. LESLIE. *The Death of Christopher Marlowe.* Harvard University Press, 1925.

JOURDAIN, CHARLES. *Recherches sur les traductions latines d'Aristote.* Paris, 1843.

KRAEMER, WOLFGANG. "Ein seltener Druck des Traktats 'De tribus impostoribus, 1598,'" *Zeitschrift für Bücherfreunde,* N.F., XIV (1922), 101–11.

LANGE, F. A. *The History of Materialism.* New York, 1925.

LECHLER, G. *Geschichte des englischen Deismus.* Stuttgart, 1841.

LECKY, W. E. H. *History of the Rise and Influence of Rationalism in Europe.* 2 vols. London, 1910.

MATHEWS, SHAILER, and SMITH, G. B. *A Dictionary of Religion and Ethics.* New York, 1921.

MEYER, EDWARD. *Machiavelli and the Elizabethan Drama.* Weimar, 1897.

OWEN, JOHN. *The Skeptics of the French Renaissance.* New York, 1893.

————. *The Skeptics of the Italian Renaissance.* London, 1893.

PEASE, A. S. "The Conclusions of Cicero's 'De natura deorum,'" *Transactions of the American Philological Association,* XLIV (1913), 25–37.

PELLISSIER, GEORGES. *La vie et les œuvres de Du Bartas.* Paris, 1882.

PINEAU, J. B. *Érasme; sa pensée religieuse.* Paris, 1924.

PLATTARD, JEAN. *L'œuvre de Rabelais (sources, invention, et composition).* Paris, 1910.

READ, CONYERS. *Sir Francis Walsingham.* 3 vols. Harvard University Press, 1925.

RENAN, ERNEST. *Averroès et l'Averroïsme.* Paris, 1882.

REUTER, H. F. *Geschichte der religiösen Aufklärung.* Berlin, 1875.

RITTER, A. H. *Geschichte der christlichen Philosophie.* 4 vols. Hamburg, 1841–45.

ROBERTSON, J. M. *A Short History of Free Thought.* 2 vols. London, 1914–15.

ROBINSON, J. H. "Petrarch's Account of Certain Averroists," *Translations and Reprints from the Original Sources of European History* (University of Pennsylvania, 1897), III, 9–10.

SANDERS, CHAUNCEY E. *Greene's Last Years.* Unpublished doctoral dissertation of the University of Chicago, 1926.

SCHWARZ, BERNHARD. *Lukians Verhältnis zum Skeptizismus.* Inaugural dissertation, Königsberg, 1914.

SEEBOHM, FREDERIC. *The Oxford Reformers*. London, 1887.

SEEMAN, MARGARETE. *Sir John Davies: Sein Leben und seine Werke*. Wien, 1913.

SMITH, PRESERVED. *A History of Modern Culture*. New York, 1930.

SNEATH, E. H. *Philosophy in Poetry: A Study of Sir John Davies's Poem "Nosce Teipsum."* New York, 1903.

STROWSKI, FORTUNAT. *De Montaigne à Pascal*. 3 vols. Paris, 1907.

STRYPE, JOHN. *Annals of the Reformation*. 4 vols. Clarendon Press, 1824.

———. *History of the Life and Acts of Edmund Grindal*. 1st ed., 1700. Clarendon Press, 1821.

———. *Life and Acts of Archbishop Whitgift*. Clarendon Press, 1822.

———. *The Life of Sir John Cheke*. London, 1705.

———. *Memorials of Thomas Cranmer*. 1st ed., 1693. London, 1853.

SYMONDS, JOHN A. *Sir Philip Sidney*. New York, 1887.

TANNENBAUM, SAMUEL A. *The Assassination of Christopher Marlowe*. New York, 1928.

———. *The Booke of Sir Thomas Moore*. New York, 1927.

THÉRY, G. *Autour du décret de 1210*, Vol. I: *David de Dinant*: Vol. II: *Alexandre d'Aphrodise*. Kaim (Belgique), 1925.

VILLEY-DESMESERETS, PIERRE. *Les sources et l'évolution des essais de Montaigne*. 2 vols. Paris, 1908.

WALSER, ERNST. *Studien zur Weltanschauung der Renaissance*. Basel, 1920.

WEBB, CLEMENT C. J. "Shakespeare and Religion," *Hibbert Journal*, XXVI (1927–28), 341–54.

WEISSBERGER, L. ARNOLD. "Machiavelli and Tudor England," *Political Science Quarterly*, XLII (1927), 589–607.

WILSON, J. DOVER. *John Lyly*. Cambridge University Press, 1905.

WINCKLER, H. A. *Der Stoïcismus eine Wurzel des Christenthums*. Berlin, 1878.

ZANTA, LÉONTINE. *La renaissance du stoïcisme au XVIᵉ siècle*. Paris, 1914.

INDEX OF NAMES

INDEX OF NAMES